Bill Neese

S0-CPQ-433

Your Family

Your Family

by

John MacArthur, Jr.

MOODY PRESS
CHICAGO

Titles Available in the Moody Elective Series:

© 1982, 1983 by
THE MOODY BIBLE INSTITUTE
OF CHICAGO
All rights reserved. No part of this book may be repro
duced in any form without permission in writing from
the publisher, except in the case of brief quotations embodied in critical articles or reviews.

All Scripture quotations in this book are from the *New
American Standard Bible,* © 1960, 1962, 1963, 1968,
1971, 1972, 1973, 1975, and 1977 by the Lockman Foundation, and are used by permission.

ISBN: 0-8024-0257-7

4 5 Printing/AF/Year 87 86 85

Printed in the United States of America

With profound gratitude to my blessed God for the sweetest, most cherished of all His expressions of love in this life— Patricia, my wife, and our children, Matthew, Marcy, Mark, and Melinda. They continually fill my heart with joy.

CONTENTS

PREFACE

For many in our time, marriage and family life have become painfully unfulfilling. Our troubled generation staggers along in the darkness of selfishness and broken relationships like a drunk in the night.

Here and there it clings to a lamppost, which dispels a little of the blackness, but rarely does it ever find the full, warm sunlight and sobriety of God's intended joy.

Psychologists, psychiatrists, counselors, and sociologists inside and outside the church offer a massive library of suggestions and solutions. But even though they light the lamps with their most excellent efforts, the drunkenness and darkness seem to be deepening.

God made man, woman, marriage, and the family. And He alone can take away the confusion, dispel the darkness, and put the light of unselfish love in the world of His creation.

All efforts to save the family must, then, depend

on that divine light. So we turn to the Bible, and especially Ephesians 5:18—6:4. There we find God's pattern for the family.

My purpose is not to suggest psychological, emotional, or functional ideas to put up a few more lampposts. I am committed, rather, to see God turn on the biblical daylight and restore complete sobriety to marriage and the family.

The solution comes not with a few mere external suggestions, but a rebuilding of the very basis of thinking. And God has clearly revealed that thinking in His Word.

It may disturb you to be brought face to face with God's design for the family. But His guarantee is that if you will bow to its power and promise, no matter how it violates the world's thinking, you will come into the blazing sunlight of full joy in those most intimate and essential relationships.

So, prayerfully, with your Bible in hand, for the sake of God's glory, the next generation's holiness, and your joy—study with me this greatest of all truth for the family.

Part One

God's Pattern for Relationships

Do not get drunk with wine, for that is dissipation, but be filled with the Spirit, speaking to one another in psalms and hymns and spiritual songs, singing and making melody in your heart to the Lord; always giving thanks for all things in the name of our Lord Jesus Christ to God, even the Father; and be subject to one another in the fear of Christ.
—Ephesians 5:18-21

1

A Place to Start

No one needs to tell us that our generation may be watching the death of marriage and an attempt to obliterate the family as we know it. Many things have contributed to that attempted homicide being committed against God's basic unit of society: immorality, adultery, fornication, homosexuality, abortion, sterilization, women's liberation, juvenile delinquency, crime, and sexual rebellion. All those things are like strands in a cord that is strangling the family. Surprisingly, opinions vary about whether this remaking of the family is good or bad. Some say that marriage and the traditional family structure *ought* to change.

I once had the privilege of going to the hospital to pick up a baby for a couple who were to adopt it. While I was there a nurse said to me, "You know, it really doesn't matter anymore who the parents are. It has no bearing on the child anyway."

I was shocked, so I asked her, "You mean you

don't think it's important that there be a loving father and mother in the home?"

"No, that really isn't the issue at all," she replied.

"Do you think it's important for a child to have a strong spiritual influence and model in his parents?"

"No, I don't know that that matters."

Much of our society has a frightening mentality about marriage and the family. Having lost their base of authority, they are groping to figure out how to make human relationships meaningful in a culture that is disintegrating. With all the confusion, it is time to reiterate the divine pattern for marriage and family living. And the revival of the family has to begin in the church, because the world's confusion on marriage and the family has made itself at home in the Body of Christ. I believe God has a standard that can make marriage and the family what they ought to be if we as Christians follow it. Then we can reach the world.

If the family is not preserved, all of society will collapse; it is inevitable. The family is the basic unit of human society. When it crumbles everything will come crashing down with it, because man will have lost the ability to pass on any meaningful thing to the emerging generation. With no common ground of communication and discipline, every generation carries within it the seeds of its own destruction.

THE BASIS OF FULFILLMENT

The presupposition. We need to recognize a basic presupposition: in order to know the divine pattern that can make a marriage and family life meaningful, in order to establish a home that can bring security, one must be a Christian. It needs to be said at the beginning that if you are not a Christian there is little hope you can make your marriage and family what God intended them to be. That does not mean that people who are not Christians can't have meaningful relationships. They can—up to a point. But they will never know total fulfillment, because as an individual finds fulfillment only in a relationship with God, so also a family finds fulfillment only in Him.

The family is designed and authored by God Himself. He is the one who created us, He invented the family and marriage, and He has written the book on how it is to function. But there is no reason to follow His guidelines, no constraint, if we have no commitment to Him. It all begins with salvation.

The power. But there's more to it than just the basic relationship, because a lot of Christians know the Lord Jesus Christ, but they are not living according to His moral law, His marital law, or His family law. Why? Because they are not filled with the Holy Spirit. It is one thing to possess the Spirit of God, to be a believer, but a necessary second dimension can be discovered in Ephesians 5:18: "And do not get drunk with wine, for that is dissipation, but be filled with the Spirit."

A story from Greek mythology can help to give us a picture of the power of this verse. A brief look at this fantasy will offer a fresh perception of what Paul is saying.

Pagan mythology taught that the great god Zeus

gave birth to a son—in a rather unusual way. The child was snatched from his mother Semele's womb while she was being incinerated before the burning glory of Zeus, whom she insisted on seeing. The child-god was then sown into the thigh of Zeus until the time came for him to be born. He was destined by Zeus to be a world ruler, but when finally born he was kidnapped by the envious Titans, the sons of earth, and killed in a gruesome fashion. Zeus came to the rescue and salvaged the heart of the child-god. Soon the child was reborn as Dionysius. Zeus then blasted the Titans with lightning, and from their ashes mankind arose. Dionysius then spawned a religion of ecstasy and emotionalism which saturated the Graeco-Roman world. The worship involved sacrifices, atrocities, perversions, and orgies, all set to music and dancing and induced by drunkenness. He became known as "the god of wine" (his Roman name was Bacchus) and was even addressed with "come thou, Savior."

Drunkenness, then, became the key to their worship. It dulled the senses sufficiently to quiet the conscience, dispel anxiety and guilt over such vile behavior, and give them a false exhilaration that counterfeited true joy. They believed that wine induced the necessary state of ecstasy and enthusiasm which lifted the worshiper to a level of communion with the gods that was otherwise impossible.

This corrupt perspective was no doubt influential in the world of the Ephesians. So Paul uses it for his marvelous contrast. He compares these dionysiac orgies of drunkenness and evil with the serene, sweet, and holy joy, power, communion, and worship that comes by being filled not with wine but with the Holy Spirit of God. We are not called to lose control through wine and find a false communion, but to be controlled by the Holy Spirit and find the true communion with God's peace and power. And we are to be constantly controlled by the Holy Spirit. as the form of the verb indicates.

Every Christian possesses the Holy Spirit but is not always controlled by, or filled with, the Spirit. Consequently, we have family and marital problems in the church. A disobedient or fleshly believer will have discord in his family just as he will have discord in his own heart, because there is discord between himself and God. Being a Christian is definitely the starting point, but being controlled by the Spirit makes the ideal a reality.

The problem is not a lack of information. Have you noticed that we're drowning in a sea of marriage information today—marriage seminars, marriage conferences, marriage encounters, marriage books, and marriage counselors *ad infinitum, ad nauseaum?* And many people think the first thing to do when they have a marital problem is go see a counselor, visit a psychiatrist or an analyst, collect a pile of books, go to a seminar, listen to tapes, learn some sure-fire principles, or whatever. I don't want to oversimplify the matter, but a person can do *all* of those things, and if he is not filled with the Spirit none of it is effective! When the Holy Spirit fills a life He controls all relationships. And then those activities can provide helpful principles on how the power of the Holy Spirit can work itself out in right relationships.

It is not my intention to develop fully the richness of this principle, but only to say that the point is this: the *sine qua non* of the Christian life is to be filled or controlled by the Holy Spirit, and only when we do that will our families be what God wants them to be.

All the teaching on family in Ephesians 5 flows from the power of the Spirit in verse 18. The filling of the Holy Spirit produces at least three results. The first is directed generally *toward ourselves,* in verse 19: "Speaking to [yourselves] in psalms and hymns and spiritual songs, singing and making melody with your heart to the Lord." The first thing a Spirit-filled person should possess is a sense of inner peace, inner contentment, inner joy that results in song. That wellspring comes from an inward sense that all is well, and bursts forth in the joy of the Lord.

The second result is directed *toward God:* "Always giving thanks for all things in the name of our Lord Jesus Christ to God, even the Father" (v. 20). A Spirit-controlled person not only sings within himself, but gives thanks to God as well. Our thanks is always to God. Even when we are genuinely thankful to another person, we should thank the Lord for working through that person, so that God is always the object of our thanks. Paul often begins his letters this way: "I thank my God in all my remembrance of you" (Philippians 1:3).

Verse 21 reveals a third result of a Spirit-filled life, *toward others:* "And [submitting] to one another in the fear of Christ." When a person has reverence and fear and stands in awe of God, and when he really worships Him, that person will be one who submits to others. Submission is vital both in the family and in the church. James 4:1 says, "What is the source of quarrels and conflicts among you? Is not the source your pleasures that wage war in your members?" Conflicts come because we won't submit; we want to get the upper hand, we want our rights, we want our way, we want our opinion to dominate. But the Spirit-filled life is not a fight for the top, it is a fight for the *bottom!* It is every man looking out not for his own interests but for the interests of others (Philippians 2:4). Throughout Scripture we are called upon to submit to one another (1 Corinthians 16:16; Hebrews 13:17; 1 Peter 2:13; 5:5).

So Paul adds this necessary dimension for the believer: the offering of praise and thanksgiving to God as a basic consequence that flows from a life controlled by the Holy Spirit. His focus is on seeking to give to God, rather than simply receiving from Him. It requires utter unselfishness to cultivate that divine perspective in everything. As someone has said, "Earth is crammed with heaven and every common bush aflame with God." We must live so that God is constantly in our sight, not only through the Scriptures but in everything. The believer must learn to hear the voice of God and see His hand in every action and circumstance, every fragrant flower, each rock and mountain, every babbling brook, the gentle slap of the surf, the blazing sky, the bending trees, and the whistling wind. Everything in life is a gift of God's love, and is an opportunity to see and praise Him. The heart must be transformed into a sanctuary where God is worshiped in all actions, circumstances, events, and people.

Where there is the control of the Holy Spirit and a worshiping heart there will be the right foundation for the family, and that brings us back to the real key—submission. And submission will only occur in a heart that is controlled by the Holy Spirit and flowing with praise to God. It is the secret to all right and fulfilling relationships.

THE CONCEPT OF SUBMISSION

Submission explained. The word *submit—hupotassō* (*hupo*, "under;" *tassō*, "to line up, to get in order, to be arranged")—means "to get in order under something." In a military sense the idea is "to rank beneath, to rank under." As Christians we are to rank ourselves under one another. The whole mentality of the Christian life as we relate to each other should be one of humility and submissiveness.

Submission examined. Now you may be saying, "But what about the elders and pastors of the church who are supposed to lead? Since we are to submit to them (Hebrews 13:17), should they also submit to us?" Yes. In terms of structure and function we are to submit to them in the church, but in terms of interpersonal relationships there is to be *mutual* submission. Of course there is submission to authority in the church, just as there is submission to authority in government and in the home, but that in no way negates the responsibility of our submission to one another on a personal level. That is exactly what the apostle Paul is really after here. The principle of submission is the theme of Ephesians 5.

Notice what Paul uses to illustrate the truth of mutual submission: the family. That is why Ephesians 5:22—6:4 deals with the family. It illustrates the thesis of verse 21, because we might read about submission and ask ourselves, "What is he talking about? What does he mean, *'submit to one another'*?" He invites us to take a look at the microcosm of the family to see the application of the principle of mutual submission. Each relationship in the family is explored. We see wives addressed in 5:22-24, husbands in verses 25-33, children in 6:1-3, and finally in verse 4, Paul speaks to parents.

Note how submission works, beginning with verse 22: "Wives, [submit yourselves] to your own husbands, as to the Lord." I find it interesting to note that the verb *submit* does not appear in the original manuscript in verse 22. It is only implied. That might surprise you. What is the significance of its omission? He is pointing out that everyone is to practice submission—not just the wives. In verse 25, he goes on to remind husbands of their responsibility to their wives. In what way is a husband to respond to his wife? Keep reading in verse 25: "Just as Christ also loved the church and gave Himself up for her." There is no greater act of submission than to die for someone, and that is precisely the way we husbands are to treat our wives. A husband is to do for his wife what Christ did for the church: He gave Himself for us in history's greatest act of submission. He bore our sins, He took our place, and He died for us.

A husband's submission to his wife does not mean that he abdicates his responsibility of leadership in the home, but that he helps her to bear her burdens, he "gets underneath" to carry her cares, he's always ready to meet her needs and to sacrifice his own desires for what helps fulfill those needs. And the children are to submit too, in obedience to their parents. But do you want to see something more? *Parents* are also to submit (Ephesians 6:4). The word translated "fathers" can mean "parents," and parents are to submit by "not provok[ing] your children to anger; but bring[ing] them up in the discipline and instruction of the Lord." That means you are to "get under" your child, as it were, and be a caring, supportive teacher.

We are all submitting at some point. Wives are to submit to the loving leadership of their husbands. Husbands are called to bow to the needs of their wives. A father has to bend to the sensitivity and needs of his child so that he does not provoke the child to anger. Every family member is an illustration of submission. There are homes where the husband understands the wife's submission but has no idea what it means for him to submit to her needs, to sacrifice himself for her. He's missed the point of Ephesians 5—it calls us all at some point to submit to everyone else in the circle of our relationships.

So before we emphasize the authority in the family we are faced with a beautiful mutuality in marriage. Compare 1 Corinthians 7. Verses 1 and 2 set the background: "Now concerning the things about which you wrote, it is good for a man not to touch a woman. But because of immoralities, let each man have his own wife, and let each woman have her own husband." Paul is answering some of their questions about the issues of marriage and the marital relationships. The key idea is in verse 3: "Let the husband fulfill his duty to his wife, and likewise also the wife to her husband." Both partners in a marriage are to submit by fulfilling each other's needs. Do you see the mutuality there? Verse 4 continues, "The wife does not have authority over her own body but the husband does; and likewise also the husband does not have authority over his own body but the wife does." There is mutuality in marriage, a beautiful mutuality that does not negate the need for leadership but recognizes the mutual submission that must characterize a marriage, and a family, at every point.

Submission illustrated. The principle of submission is illustrated in many ways. Men and women are equal in the sight of God, according to Galatians 3:28: "There is neither male nor female; for you are all one in Christ Jesus." There is no second-class spiritual citizenship. Before God, there is only oneness; a man is not spiritually superior to a woman in any way. The best illustration of that is found in 1 Corinthians 11:3, which says it in a very graphic way: "But I want you to understand that Christ is the head of every man, and the man is the head of a woman." That should be obvious—within the home there has to be leadership, and by God's design the head of the woman is the man. But read on: "And God is the head of Christ."

That is interesting. Does Paul mean to say that God is *superior* to Christ? Not at all. Are they not one? Didn't Jesus say, "If you have seen Me you have seen the Father"? "I and the Father are one"? What about John 1:1?

In what way, then, is God the Father the head of Christ? Never in essence (or nature), but only in function. Within the function of the Godhead it was deemed necessary that Christ should submit Himself to the Father. The same Jesus who said, "All authority has been given to Me in heaven and on earth" (Matthew 28:19) also said, "My food is to do the will of Him who sent me" (John 4:34). In their nature or essence the members of the Trinity are equal, but by God's design their functions demanded that the Son submit to the Father in a selfless humiliation. Does that make us think less of the Son? Of course not; it makes us think more highly of Him! It is part of His wondrous beauty.

Now here's the point: the same kind of structure is necessary in marriage. The partners' spiritual natures are the same, their positions before God are equal, but in order for the family to function in harmony, the woman, with no loss of dignity, takes the place of submission to the headship of her husband. Her tenderness and gentleness, given by God, are to come alongside to support the strength of the man. The issue is not superiority or inferiority. Mutual submission in marriage blends without confusion or contradiction with the concepts of headship and authority. As she submits to follow, so he submits to lead her. Both authority and submission are still preserved, which is essential for proper function in marriage.

In the realm of government we also see authority and submission. Romans 13:1 says that the powers that be are "established by God." He knows that we cannot have human government without authority and submission. Further, verse 4 says that the government "does not bear the sword for nothing." In other words, God has given policemen, the military, and other governmental agencies authority, and that is why Peter says we are to submit to every law of man, to the king, to governors, and to everyone in authority over us (2 Peter 2:13-18). Why? Because God knows that society is maintained on the basis of authority and submission. And it is not necessarily godly men who are in authority. Submission to authority does not imply either a spiritual, intellectual, or essential inequality—the Scriptures are simply speaking of *function*.

Probably the largest single unit of human relationships is the national government. Nations must function with authority. There will be kings, governors, police, soldiers, and other leaders, and there will be those of us who follow their leadership (cf. 1 Peter 3). Is it because they are superior to everyone else? No! There simply has to be authority and submission or else anarchy, and no society can survive anarchy.

In the smallest unit of human relationships, the

family, the same principle holds true. There cannot be anarchy in a family, with no one responsible for discipline, earning wages, controlling behavior, or giving direction, without creating chaos. And chaos is precisely what exists in American families today. The dissolution of the family is the beginning of the dissolution of the nation, the beginning of anarchy. Mankind cannot function apart from the principle of authority and submission. God has designed things that way, and only as we rely on His Word and His power can we make marriage and the family the blessing He intended.

THE DEMISE OF MARRIAGE

Today's marriages. I believe that the message of Ephesians 5:21—6:4 is one we particularly need to hear today. I'm deeply concerned about the future of marriage. We are being told that about half of the couples who get married each year end up in divorce courts. Of course the epidemic of divorce also contributes to many other problems, such as loneliness, poverty, unwanted children, or children living in broken families.

Abortion is as common now among married as among unmarried people. One-third of all couples of child-bearing age are now sterile. Couples are choosing not to have children. Why? Selfishness. In too many cases it is only because children complicate things; they tend to get in the way. If a couple has no children, they can dissolve the marriage and leave much easier. How tragic! The result of all this is a generation of children growing up in decimated families, saying, "The *last* thing I want to do is get married. I don't want to repeat that mess." Many have had chaotic and totally unfulfilled family lives, and they want out. There exists a serious lack of commitment to others. A society is forming based totally on selfish desires. The children of our generation's crumbling marriages are looking for cheaper options than marriage, so when the thrill burns off they can find another person to rekindle it. Even some marriages that manage to hang together are characterized by unfaithfulness, loss of respect and trust, pride, self-centeredness, materialism, laziness, and loneliness.

And those marital and family problems have crept into the church as well. The answer is not more marriage counselors, marriage seminars, or books on marriage. We need to back up to our point of origin in Ephesians 5:18: "Be filled with the Spirit." When we make that a reality, God Himself will produce within us those virtues that make for a meaningful marriage. We have been great at sticking Band-Aids on symptoms, but God's principles for marriage and family living in Ephesians 5:21—6:4 meet reality head-on. The same was true in Paul's day. Let's step back for a moment and examine those cultural conditions that he challenged. It will open the passage up to our understanding.

Marriage in Paul's day. The Jews of Paul's day had a rather low view of women. To them women were just like slaves. In fact, the morning prayer of a Jewish man might be, "God, I thank you that I'm not a Gentile, a slave, or a woman." Divorce had long been common. In Deuteronomy 24:1 Moses describes a man who married a woman and she lost favor with him because he found uncleanness in her. He wrote her a bill of divorce and sent her away. Apparently, if there was any uncleanness on the wife's part, divorce was commonly sought. Of course, everything hinged on what "uncleanness" involved.

One rabbi said that only adultery could be suitable grounds for divorce under the term *uncleanness*. But another rabbi said "uncleanness" could be anything, and Rabbi Hillel taught that a wife was unclean if she spoiled her husband's dinner or put too much salt on it. If she burned the bagels, talked with men in the streets, or said something against her mother-in-law, that was enough! Rabbi Akiba even insisted that if a man found a woman who was prettier than his wife, the latter became unclean in his eyes. He could write her a bill of divorce, send her out, and marry the pretty one. So the people of Israel were offered two views of when it was acceptable to end a marriage: for adultery only, or for almost anything. Which view do you think they accepted? The second one. By the time Paul began preaching, the Jews were divorcing their wives almost at will. That wasn't what the Bible taught, but that was the corruption that came about. We will examine closely the questions of divorce and remarriage in later chapters.

The pagan Greek world was even worse. In fact, there was no legal procedure for divorce in Greek society, since wives were simply the ones who cleaned the house and bore legitimate children. Men found their sexual enjoyment outside of marriage, so they didn't bother to divorce their wives. The Athenian orator Demosthenes said, "We have courtesans for the sake of pleasure, we have concubines for the sake of daily cohabitation, and we have wives for the purpose of having children legitimately and being faithful guardians for our household affairs."

That is why Paul, writing in the midst of the Greek culture, refers so often to *porneia*, "fornication." Fornication was very much a part of Greek society. The word *pornē* means "a woman for sale," and the word *pornos* means "a man for sale." Female and male prostitution were rampant in the Greek world because people found their sexual pleasure outside of marriage. In addition, historians note that Athenian society was also dominated by pedophilia, which is sexual abuse of children. Paul faced that as well.

Divorce in the Jewish community was common. Prostitution, homosexuality, lesbianism, and pedophilia abounded in the Greek world. And we are not surprised to learn that the Romans' view of marriage was just a culmination of all this earlier perversion. Jerome, an ancient writer, tells us of one Roman woman who married her twenty-third husband, and she was his twenty-first wife! Marriage in Roman times became little more than legalized prostitution. There was also a strong women's liberation movement. Women didn't want to have children, because they thought it hurt the appearance of their bodies. Some of them wanted to be able to do everything that men did, so they developed women wrestlers, women sword-throwers, and so on. One writer, Juvenal, says the women began to lord it over their husbands, but before long they would vacate the home and flit from one marriage to another, "wearing out their bridal veils!"

So now we understand that when Paul said, "Wives, [submit yourselves] to your own husbands, as to the Lord. . . . Husbands, love your wives, just as Christ also loved the church," he was not simply reminding them of something they already knew. He was saying, "Listen. This is a call to a new standard of living. I'm telling you to live in a way you don't know anything about." He was calling on them to rebel against their culture. Those new believers in Ephesus and everywhere else this letter was read had come out of that chaotic culture, and Paul was telling wives to give themselves to their husbands and husbands to give themselves to their wives as Christ gave Himself to His church. That was devastating, dynamic new information. The Christian home was to be a place where authority and submission were so couched in love that they melted together in the mutuality of love and respect. That is the divine standard. Let me illustrate it for you from the Old Testament love song.

Marriage as God designed it. The Song of Solomon contains a beautiful picture of a right marriage relationship. You don't sense an obvious authority and an obvious submission. All you see is a beautiful, tender love, with authority and submission quietly at work. In the biblical record, the great king is married to the Shulamite woman, and they are deeply in love. Notice each of their functions in the marriage.

In Song of Solomon 2:3-16, the Shulamite describes her husband as the head of the home. She pictures him as her protector in verse 3. Here is a woman finding shelter, protection, security, confidence, comfort, and rest in her husband. That is a recognition of his headship, but it all flows from their love, and there is nothing threatening there—no one has to "knuckle under." He is also her provider (v. 4), her sustainer (v. 5), her security (v. 6), and her leader and initiator (vv. 10-15). Her husband takes the lead, and there is no oppression or dictatorial spirit in the passage. In fact, this section closes with a beautiful statement. Even though she sees him as her protector, provider, sustainer, security, and her leader and initiator, she says in verse 16, "My beloved is mine and I am his." The relationship never loses its mutuality.

In chapter 5, the Shulamite woman responds to her husband's strength and leadership with a marvelous portrait of him through her eyes of love. He is ruddy and handsome (v. 10). His skin is bronzed, and his eyes are soft and tender (vv. 11-12). There is color in his cheeks, and his lips are fragrant (v. 13). His hands are like gold (that is, bronzed), and his stomach and legs are muscular and strong (vv. 14-15*a*). She sees him as handsome and rugged but also with character. According to verse 16, when he opens his mouth he isn't crass or rude. Then at the end of the verse she says, "This is my beloved and this, my friend." I love that. She doesn't see him as a dictator but as a beloved friend. There is the mutuality again. When love bathes a relationship, everything fits together.

But even in a relationship like that, they faced a problem. According to chapter 5, verse 1, the husband came home late at night, after his wife had already gone to bed. He was full of love for her, and he knocked on the door, asking her to let him in (v. 2). Notice her response in the next verse. She refused him because she didn't want to be bothered. But when she heard his hand on the door, love welled up in her heart, and she was sorry for her lack of submission. So she arose and went to the door, but it was too late (vv. 5-6). Her "beloved" was gone. He didn't force himself: you see, he was submissive, too—to her.

She began to panic and went running all over the city trying to find him (v. 7, cf. 6:1). Finally in chapter 6 she found him in the garden, and rather than being angry with her, he confirmed his love to her. And the problem was solved, as they renewed their love.

We need to understand what the Bible has to say about a meaningful marriage relationship. There are two things to keep in mind: (1) We all are to submit to one another in a beautiful mutuality; (2) Functionally, there has to be authority and submission. When we learn the fullness of those two dimensions of truth, our families are going to be what God wants them to be. It isn't easy because to apply these truths is to go upstream against the current of our Christless culture and human nature. We can be successful only to the degree we are transformed by the Lord Jesus Christ and controlled by the Holy Spirit.

QUESTIONS FOR DISCUSSION

1. How has our society's view of marriage deteriorated over the past few decades?
2. Why does a person have to be a Christian in order to fulfill God's intention for marriage?
3. How is being filled with the Spirit compared to drunkenness in Ephesians 5:18? What three results should the filling of the Spirit produce in our lives?
4. What does the Greek word for "submit" literally mean? What is the difference between submission to authority and mutual submission to one another?
5. How were women viewed in ancient times? Why was divorce common among the Jews of Paul's day?
6. The Song of Solomon describes a beautiful marriage relationship. List some of the characteristics of that ideal relationship.

Part Two

God's Pattern
for Wives

Wives, be subject to your own husbands, as to the Lord. For the husband is the head of the wife, as Christ also is the head of the church, He Himself being the Savior of the body. But as the church is subject to Christ, so also the wives ought to be to their husbands in everything.
— Ephesians 5:22-24

2

Submission, Not Slavery

In Ephesians 5:21 the apostle Paul has established the foundational principle of mutual submission, which is to characterize marriage and family life. We have seen briefly that the mutuality of loving sacrifice exists in harmony with, not in opposition to, the concepts of headship and submission that God has ordained for the smooth functioning of the family. Verse 21 serves as a "front door" that opens to specific directives addressed to wives, husbands, children, and parents in 5:22—6:4. With the background set, Paul moves to teach the duty of the wife in verses 22-24.

THE MATTER OF SUBMISSION

We have already seen that the Greek word for "submit" *(hupotassō)* is not part of the original of verse 22, but is implied from its use in verse 21 (it is used in the parallel text in Colossians 3:18). The word is a functional term that refers to "lining up underneath" and in no way implies a difference in essence. Note also that Paul does not use the word *obey (hupakouō)* in addressing wives. Paul reserves *hupakouō* for children (6:1) and slaves (6:5), but a wife is not a slave, standing in the center of the house awaiting commands: "Do this!" "Get that!" "Go over there!" "Fix me that!" The marriage relationship is much more intimate, personal, and vital than that, as indicated by the words "your own husband." There is both singular devotion and a possessiveness in that phrase, which assumes that a wife would willingly respond in submission to her *own* husband—one whom she possesses. Such possessive submission denies any inferiority on her part, and points up again the God-ordained distinction in function so that order in marriage can be preserved.

That distinction in function was introduced back in Genesis 3:16, when God said: "Yet your desire shall be for your husband, and he shall rule over you." In Genesis 2:24 God also said that the two (husband and wife) would be one flesh. Yet, in response to her unique creation by God, a wife is to be submissive to the headship of her husband, not as a slave, but as one who is provided for, cared for, and secured by her husband. And her subjection is not a matter of what she does for him apart from what he is responsible to do for her.

Headship belongs to the man. Physically, God designed men to be stronger in order to work for, protect, provide for, and give security to the wife, whom the Holy Spirit calls the "weaker vessel" (1 Peter 3:7). Man is the stronger partner, the protector and provider. God designed it that way from creation.

In Colossians 3:18, the parallel passage to Ephesians 5:22, Paul says basically the same thing but uses a word there that is very important: "Wives, be subject to your husbands, as is fitting in the Lord." The phrase "as is fitting" is the verb *anekō*, which means "to be fitting, seemly, or proper." In the Septuagint (the Greek translation of the Old Testament), *anekō* is used of something that is legally binding. It's also used in the legal sense in verse 8 of Philemon. Paul is saying that the wife's submission to her husband is in a sense *legally binding*—it's the accepted law of human society.

Where does a human society get its law? Historically, any society that acknowledged God at all formulated laws that were basically restatements of divine principles. We are seeing such divine foundations eroded in our society, and now men determine morality by majority vote. But a look into history will show for the most part that laws governing societies in which God had any influence were laws that had a biblical base. For example, we have laws against murder, theft, sexual evil, perjury, and so on. Those laws come directly from the moral code of the Ten Commandments, found in Exodus 20. We have enacted laws commensurate with God's revelation. So the point is that for a wife to submit to her husband is both fitting and proper—not only because of the divinely created order but also because the best in past society has confirmed its obligatory design.

I recognize that this issue of authority and submission is not popular. This generation has trouble accepting God's principles because they are a society victimized by a nonbiblical philosophy of living and thinking. Much of today's thinking can be traced back to the leaders of the French Revolution, who advocated a humanistic, egalitarian approach to life. They wanted a society with absolute equality, a sexless, classless, godless kind of humanistic existence. Such ideas have been brewing for generations, and now our age is drinking the bitter product. And the church, instead of rejecting that philosophy, has fallen prey to it, pushing for equal status for everyone, and trying to erase all distinctions in the ministry of the Body. Such a philosophy forces a wrong interpretation on the Bible in modern terms rather than accepting the clear teaching of the Word of God. A return to the authoritative Word to examine several key passages will clarify the matter of submission.

1 Peter 3:1-6. First Peter 3:1 reads: "In the same way, you wives, be submissive to your own husbands." Here, again, is the word *hupotassō*. Remember, it means "to come under in rank" and is a function word, not an essence word. It refers to how leadership should function in the home. And Peter also emphasizes the possessiveness that softens the submissive role ("your own husbands"). In other words, because the husband is the wife's possession, submission should be a very welcome response.

Peter continues verse 1 by saying: "So that even if any of them are disobedient to the word, they may be won without a word by the behavior of

their wives." I'm glad Peter said that, because inevitably someone will say, "Look, you don't understand my husband. He's not a Christian, and he
doesn't obey God or His Word. How can I submit
to this man?" That person is precisely the one to
whom this verse speaks. If a husband doesn't obey
the Word, submit—*submit anyway.* And without
your saying anything, he may be won. Instead of
writing "Repent" on the bottom of his beer cans,
pasting little notes in his lunch pail, or leaving him
a gospel tract, if a wife orders her life in conformi-
ty with God's pattern for marriage she may, without even using the Word, win her husband by her
behavior.

You may be asking, "What kind of behavior?"
According to verse 2 it must be "chaste and re-
spectful." A wife should have respect for her husband. Not only is her life to be chaste (pure behavior, pure conduct, pure living), but also she is to
have a reverence, a sense of awe (which is a spirit
of genuine humility) for her husband.

When a wife is concerned with her husband,
when she respects him and her conduct is chaste,
her attitude will manifest itself in her outward activity. "And let not your adornment be external
only—braiding the hair, and wearing gold jewelry,
and putting on dresses" (v. 3). Our society is so
preoccupied with those things they have almost
become a curse. But a woman who preoccupies
herself with all the external adornment is in violation of the biblical standard. Why? Because a
woman who is submissive doesn't call attention to
herself.

Instead of consuming interest in the external, verse 4 says a woman should be concerned with "the hidden person of the heart," or "the secret of the heart" (the word *person* is not in the original). In other words, don't work on the outside, work on the inside. I'm not advocating that women ignore their appearance (the submissive wife will wish to be outwardly lovely to bring joy to her husband), but that the appearance reflect the beauty of the inner spirit. And what inward virtues should characterize such a woman? She will possess "the imperishable quality of a gentle and quiet spirit" (which implies that all the apparel and gold and ornamented hair *are* perishable). "Gentle" is the Greek word *praüs*, which simply means "silent, still." That certainly sounds foreign to our society, doesn't it? But it is, nevertheless, God's standard. The Scriptures exhort women to adorn themselves in godliness, with a gentle and quiet spirit. That does not mean that wives are just to vegetate or never offer an opinion. It does mean that they understand that God expects them to be humble and still. That is the beauty and strength of a woman. And her opinions, her confrontations, her teaching offered to her husband rises from such beauty and strength.

By the way, all of this is "in the sight of God." The Greek word *enōpion* actually means "face-to-face." As a wife stands "face-to-face" with God, He does not see her hair or how much gold she is wearing; He is looking for a gentle and quiet spirit. In His sight that is "precious" *(poluteles)*. That rich word is used in Mark 13:3 when the woman opened the alabaster box and took out the priceless ointment.

A gentle and quiet spirit is precious to God—very valuable in His sight. Such virtue is priceless.

In verse 5 we are given some historical perspective: "For in this way in former times the holy women also [did]." Holiness has always been the standard, the concern of godly women, because their preoccupation is with God. Those holy women were determined to uphold God's standards. Thus they adorned themselves with a gentle and quiet spirit and were submissive to their own husbands.

Peter focuses on one such woman: "Sarah obeyed Abraham, calling him lord [a term of respect and reverence], and you have become her children if you do what is right without being frightened by any fear" (v. 6). As Abraham is the father of the faithful (Galatians 3:7), Sarah is the mother of the submissive. And notice, there was no fear involved. Many women say, "I'm afraid to submit to my husband. I'll lose my rights. He'll take advantage of me." But because those holy women trusted God they had no fear of obeying God. If there was an abuse they knew God would take care of the results. Wives, as you obey God and submit to your husbands with a gentle and quiet spirit, you can believe God that He will honor your obedience—no matter what.

1 Corinthians 11:3-12. History tells us that the city of Corinth was living with a women's liberation movement. Women were trying to do the same jobs as men, and they were wanting to look and act like men. Apparently some of the women in the church at Corinth were swept into the movement, and it was bringing a reproach to the name of Christ and His church. Paul wrote to straighten this out.

In Corinthian society women traditionally were expected to be submissive, and the veils they wore were a symbol of their submission, modesty, and humility. Only two kinds of women took their veils off: prostitutes and feminists. A prostitute took off her veil so men could see if they wanted her. The feminist removed hers as a symbol of protest. So Paul wrote to the women at Corinth and he said, in effect, "Keep your veils on. In your society, they signify submission. Now respond to that symbol, so the world does not see the church rebelling against a God-ordained principle." Paul is simply saying again that a woman is to take a place of submission and not to violate it.

Titus 2:3-5. Titus 2 is another key passage that has much to teach us. Paul writes in verse 3: "Older women [mature women whose children are probably no longer in the home] likewise are to be reverent in their behavior, not malicious gossips, nor enslaved to much wine, teaching what is good." Notice that the older women are to be teachers. And whom are they to teach? "That they may [teach] the young women" (v. 4). Here is a beautiful pattern for the life of any older woman. The mature women are to teach the younger women first, "to love their husbands" (one word in the Greek, *philandros,* "man-lover," or "husband-lover"). They should be characterized by love for their husbands.

The emphasis is often that the husband is commanded to love his wife (Ephesians 5:25) and the wife is only a responder. Some would say to the husband, "If your wife doesn't love you it's your fault: you're not loving her." That concept limps, though, because here in Titus 2:4 wives are commanded to love their husbands. Men respond to love, too! Again we see a tremendous mutuality and balance. A wife has as much responsibility to love her husband as he does to love her. That is a basic mutual responsibility.

Verse 4 also says women are "to love their children." Remember, love is *self-sacrifice*. Jesus said that the greatest act of love is giving oneself (John 15:13). Women are to do whatever has to be done to meet the needs of their husbands and children. In fact, the terms imply that the wife would even give her life for them. Young women must also be taught "to be sensible, pure, workers at home, kind, being subject to their own husbands, that the word of God may not be dishonored." That is the real issue! God wants His Word to be glorified, and when we do not live by that Word it is dishonored. Disobedience says, in effect, "Who cares what the Bible says?" If women are to honor God's Word they must love their husbands and children. Notice too the ideas of singular affection, devotion, and possession again, "their *own* husbands." The phrase "being subject" is the word *hupotassō* again, the same word for submission. So once more the Scriptures command that wives are to submit to their own husbands.

WORKING MOTHERS

I want to consider in some detail the phrase "workers at home" (v. 5). We have a problem in

America—nobody's home! Do you realize there are more than forty million working mothers in America, and that six million of them have little children? Approximately one out of every three mothers with a child under three holds a full-time job. And many who don't work are engulfed in TV or running around town. Who's raising the children and taking care of the home? In many cases, no one! I am convinced that the answer to this problem is found in women's response to the phrase "workers at home" in Titus 2:5. What does it mean? Very simply, the word *oikourgous* comes from *oikos* ("home") and *ergon* ("work"), thus "worker at home." I think the emphasis is really that wives ought to work when at home and they ought to work at home. That's not profound, is it? Yet the word confronts both laziness and abandonment. A woman may say, "But I have a wonderful job and we need the money. How can the Bible tell me to work at home?" But that is what the Bible says here. Consider its implications.

We have already noted that the word *ergon* means "work," but in New Testament Greek it involves a specific job, a task, and can be translated "employment." The word does not refer to the quality of work but to an assigned task. So a woman is to be employed in the assigned task of working at home. The use of *ergon* as an assigned employment, task, or work can be seen in the following passages: Mark 13:34; John 4:34; 17:4; Acts 13:2; Philippians 2:30; and 1 Thessalonians 5:13. Also compare 1 Timothy 5:14: "Therefore I want younger [women] to get married, bear children,

[and] keep house." So what's a wife and mother to do with her life? Pursue a career? I don't see that priority here. Clearly, according to Titus 2:3-5, a woman is to be a lover of her husband, a lover of her children, and one who does her assigned task *at home*.

All of this seems to be related to the general principle that a wife is to be submissive to her *own* husband. A woman who works outside the home has a different set of circumstances to deal with: other involvements, other complications, other bosses, other people giving the orders, and other men to whom she must submit. The boss might tell her, "That's not the way to dress. I want you to dress *this way*." So she has to buy a new wardrobe, and if her husband doesn't agree there may be conflict at that point. A woman who works outside the home puts herself under authorities that have no biblical injunction to be responsible for her as a husband does. Many of the problems in our society are directly related to the absence of women in the home.

Even secular anthropologists are recognizing the fearfully negative results in a world of working wives and mothers. Marvin Harris, writing in *Why America Changed: Our Cultural Crisis* (Simon and Schuster, 1981), lays many of the various troubles of our time at the feet of working women. He shows that the working woman is the child of consumptive materialism. The women's liberation efforts, he says, are created only to justify the materialism that took women into the money-making pursuit. These women have thereby impacted the home. He accuses them of undermining the husband's role; driving male wages down by increasing the supply of workers; destroying "the marital and procreative imperative" that hinges on women's being in the home raising children; shattering the traditional American domestic life and the way of love and sex; bringing an end to "the lifetime, male-dominated, two-parent, multichild, breadwinner family"; creating black unemployment by filling up jobs with lowpaid and unaggressive laborers, and thereby leading to an increase in the crime rate.

In the August 1981 issue of *Psychology Today,* he is quoted: "Unwittingly, therefore, white women, responding to their own economic imperatives clothed in the rhetoric of sexual liberation, are steadily tightening the vise that holds the ghetto in its jaws" (p. 42).

On the other side of the picture, Susanna Wesley once said of her commitment to the home and children: "No one can, without renouncing the world, in the most literal sense, observe my method; and there are few, if any, that would entirely devote above twenty years of the prime of life in hopes to save the souls of their children, when they think they may be saved without so much ado; for that was my principle intention."

The issue is *not* whether the children are home from school yet. A woman's obligation to her home doesn't change because her children are in school. In fact, psychological tests have shown that children who grow up in homes where the mother works are much more insecure than children whose mother is home. Even when a child is in school, if he knows his mother is home it serves as an anchor.

The whole issue of working women raises another important and related question: Is a woman ever to be the "breadwinner," the main provider for her family? I don't find in the Bible any statement that says the woman is to be the protector or the provider for the family. And, ultimately, our convictions must come not from our experience but from the authoritative Word of God. What I find in Scripture is a statement in 1 Timothy 5:8 (and here it's talking about a man): "If any one does not provide for his own, and especially for those of his household, he has denied the faith, and is worse than an unbeliever." The context here deals with widows, and the passage is teaching that the man is to provide for any widow in his own house or immediate family, but it also reaches to those in his extended family. The point is that the man is to be the provider, and adverse circumstances don't seem to change that pattern.

What about the woman with children at home whose husband dies or divorces her and she has to go to work? In such cases, the father is not there and by going to work, the mother also is absent. Who's responsible? The answer comes from the spirit of 1 Timothy 5:8, where men in the family are to provide. If I am related to such a person *I'm* responsible to help take up her support so that she can stay home. And if she has no family who can do that, the *church* is responsible. She should not have to go to work outside the home and abdicate the primary responsibility God has given her (1 Timothy 3:15).

What about older women whose children are grown? The answer is in Titus 2:3-5. When they were young women they were to be loving their husbands and children, keeping their homes, and so on. Now that they're older they should invest themselves in a spiritual ministry of teaching the younger women. I'm not saying that a woman can't work at that point, but I don't see a provision for that in Scripture. She may exercise that option if she chooses, but I do know that Scripture says the mature women are responsible to teach the younger women the things they've learned. The next generation isn't going to have any women to do that if younger women aren't staying at home and learning from those who are older. There will be no legacy to pass on.

This is the plan of the liberationist women, such as Felice Schwartz, president of Catalyst. In the *Working Woman* magazine, January 1982, she wrote: "By the year 2000, when the children of today's current generation of career women are themselves emerging from their teens, the polarization of sexes that put women in the home at the nurturing end of the spectrum and men in the office at the work end of the spectrum, will have disappeared—and with it the stereotypes of supportive women and aggressive men."

If the family is to be preserved and the next generation kept from this powerful attack, women must follow God-given priorities.

I recognize that many women don't have much

of a choice right now. Nobody is taking care of them or making provision for them. Some women are working because no one in their families is willing to provide for them. This is something the church has neglected for centuries and needs to take seriously. The woman is not to be the breadwinner. She is to care for her family.

Do you know why so many women are in the position of trying to be breadwinners today? Because young couples get married and decide to get the house they desire and the car they want. But it all is predicated on the fact that both of them will have to work. After they become accustomed to that life-style, a child is born, the mother stays home for three months, the child is given to a babysitter, the mother goes back to work, and the babysitter raises the child. We cannot approach life that way and say, "Look how the Lord has blessed us." If the husband is the provider and God blesses a family in a gracious, prosperous way, that's great. But if the wife has to violate the standard that God has ordained and leave the children to go to work for material things, don't confuse the blessing of God with disobedient presumption.

Some wife or mother may object, "I have a lot of energy and creativity, and I want to do things." Great! Go through your priorities first. The following list may help.

1. To God
—A devotion to knowing and living out His will according to His Word (Colossians 3:16; 2 Timothy 2:15).

—A dedication to walking in and by the Spirit so that the "fruit of the Spirit" is consistently manifest in my life (Ephesians 5:18ff; Galatians 5:16, 22-23).

2. To Family

—An unselfish devotion to my husband, children, and home (Titus 2:5).

—Subjecting myself to my own husband—seeing to his desires and needs over those of any other man (Titus 2:5; Colossians 3:18; Ephesians 5:22-23).

—Raising godly children (Ephesians 6:1-4; Colossians 3:20; 1 Timothy 5:10).

—Returning provision and care to my parents (1 Timothy 5:4, 16).

3. To Fellow Saints

—Teaching and discipling younger women (Titus 2:5). That includes devotion to instruction and to being an example of biblical teaching in regard to the priorities of husband and family.

—Doing good works, which include being hospitable, serving fellow saints, and caring for orphans, widows, and those in distress (1 Timothy 2:10; Proverbs 31:10-31).

In Proverbs 31:10-31 I want you to meet an industrious woman, and if you think a woman is stifled in her God-ordained role, take a close look at this amazing passage of Scripture:

• *Her value (v. 10):* "Her worth is far above jewels."

• *Her trustworthiness (v. 11):* "The heart of her

husband trusts in her, and he will have no lack of gain." Her husband can trust her with the finances without any fear that she will waste their money or squander their resources.

• *Her supportiveness (v. 12):* "She does him good and not evil all the days of her life." She sees herself as one who supports and undergirds her husband to free him from anxiety and fear.

• *Her productivity (vv. 13-14):* "She looks for wool and flax." In fact, if she has to travel like a merchant ship to bring it from afar, she does (v. 14). And according to verse 19, she puts it on the spindle and the distaff and makes thread. And with that thread she makes necessary things. She is productive!

All this comes short of saying that a woman must stay at home and never leave. She may have a ministry, disciple people, attend a Bible study, shop, and do other things that require her leaving her home. Obviously, there are things she has to do and places she has to go if she wishes to be productive.

• *Her sacrifice (v. 15):* "She rises also while it is still night, and gives food to her household, and portions to her maidens." She has more concern for her family than for her own comfort. Her primary concern is to live for her family.

• *Her enterprise (vv. 16-19):* "She considers a field and buys it." She buys the field, purchases the seed, and plants a vineyard. There is a place for enterprise, but the home is the base. The wife is not the source of the family's income. If a

family is not able to live on the husband's salary,
they may be living beyond their God-intended
means.

• *Her strength:* "She girds herself with strength,
and makes her arms strong" (v. 17). Such a woman is not frail and self-indulgent but is working
with her hands to provide the necessities of the
home, not only because they need it for the moment, but also because she's planning for the
future, against the moment when tragedy might
come (v. 25 in Hebrew says she'll laugh at the
future).

• *Her priorities (vv. 20-24):* A progression appears in these verses which spells out another
reason she does all this. "She extends her hand
to the poor" (v. 20). She does it so that she can
give to those who have nothing. She also provides scarlet clothing for her household to protect them from the cold weather (v. 21). And
when the needs of the poor and the needs of her
family are met, she makes herself a lined over-
coat out of tapestry (v. 22). It is a garment of
function and unusual beauty.

Finally, in verse 24, after she has met the needs
of the poor, her family, and herself, she starts a
little business out of her home, selling fine linen
and delivering belts to the merchant. And that,
too, is found in the right sequence of priorities.

• *Her result (vv. 27-28):* "She looks well to the
way of her household, and does not eat the bread
of idleness. Her children rise up and bless her;
her husband also, and he praises her." There is

the prize; all a result of God's perfect plan and design.

SUBMISSIVE WIVES

The manner of submission. Look briefly at the rest of Ephesians 5:22-24. The manner of submission is found in verse 22*b*: "As to the Lord." Wives, when you submit to your husband it should not be with the attitude, "I'll do it, but this is really going to be rough! If you only knew what I'm sacrificing." No. You are called to submit "as to the Lord." If Jesus Christ walked up to you and said, "Go home and take care of your husband and your children," what would you say? I hope it would be, "Yes, Lord." If your husband said that, would you do it? The Lord desires to say that through him because these are His principles and He stands in the place of leadership in your family.

The motive of submission. "For the husband is the head of the wife" (v. 23*a*). Even as Christ is the Head of the church and the Savior of the Body, so the husband is the head of the wife, and she is the body. The head, not the body, takes the lead. You say, "But that's degrading." When a body responds to its head it is not degrading; it is harmonious. If a body *doesn't* respond to its head, that is degrading. When we see a well-coordinated, functioning body, both the body and the head are honored. When the body doesn't respond, both are dishonored.

The model of submission. Read verses 23*b*-24

carefully. Who is the pattern to follow in all this? Christ the Head of the church, Christ the Savior of the Body: therefore, "As the church is subject to Christ, so also the wives ought to be to their husbands in everything." When Jesus Christ died on the cross He said, "It is finished." All we do is take His full provision. There is the illustration. Now in the home the husband is the provider, the deliverer, the protector, the savior. We don't need a co-savior or co-redeemer, or co-breadwinners and co-protectors. The wife needs to come under the protection, provision, and preservation of her husband. That is God's ordained pattern. Believe me, when we follow that pattern we will have happier homes, more godly children, and no divorces. God will be honored, and the Word of God will not be blasphemed.

Finally, verse 24 says that wives are to submit "in everything." There is only one exception. If a husband tells his wife to do something that is disobedient to God, then she has to say what Peter said, "We must obey God rather than men" (Acts 5:29). But short of that, she should submit in everything. And what is the key to all this? Back to verse 18: "Be filled with the Spirit." The Spirit-filled wife can do this, and God's Word will be honored, and she will be blessed.

QUESTIONS FOR DISCUSSION

1. Why is the word *submit* used in Ephesians 5:22 instead of the word *obey?* What is the difference between the two words?

2. In Titus 2:3-5 Paul tells the older women to teach the younger women. Is this happening today? Should it be?

3. According to Titus 2:4-5, what are the duties of the wife? What is meant by "workers at home"? Is it ever justifiable for mothers to pursue employment outside the home?

4. What qualities do Proverbs 31:10-31 attribute to the excellent wife?

5. What exception is made to the model of submission for wives (Acts 5:29)? How should a woman decide when to take that exception?

3

Sorting Out the Priorities

The standards for a Christian are different from those of the world, and that must not be forgotten. We are living as salt and light in a decaying and dark society (Matthew 5:13-16), and God calls on us to live differently. Because we are often victimized by that society, living differently is never easy. Even when God's Word speaks clearly on certain issues, it is sometimes very hard to hear, understand, and apply what He said because we have been influenced by a system that is at odds with that divine standard.

In the face of such pressure, the New Testament repeatedly calls us to a higher level of living, a different manner of life, another dimension of existence. It calls us to think, speak, and act in a new and unique way. We are to "set [our minds] on the things above, not on the things that are on earth" (Colossians 3:2); we are to "put on the new self" (Ephesians 4:24; cf. Colossians 3:10); we are to "walk in a manner worthy of the calling with which [we] have been called" (Ephesians 4:1); and we "walk no longer just as the Gentiles also walk" (Ephesians 4:17). No longer are believers to function as the world functions. In other words, we have been "transferred from the domain of darkness . . . to the kingdom of His beloved Son" (Colossians 1:13).

Our distinctive is our identification with Christ, and it is also the hope of humanity—in seeing this distinctive they themselves can be drawn to Jesus Christ. The objective, then, for the Christian, is to be unique, different, set apart—to be unlike the world. The only thing that will make one truly distinct from the world is to be filled with the Spirit of God. When a believer is filled with the things of the world there will be no difference.

This principle becomes very specific when we begin talking about the priorities of the wife.

THE JEWISH VIEW IN THE TIME OF CHRIST

In chapter 2 we looked at several passages of Scripture that indicate that a wife's and mother's priority is to be in the home. That was also the teaching of Jewish law at the time of Christ. The Jewish view serves as a helpful background and illustration of the responsibility of the wife. The Jewish view is contained in the *Mishnah,* a codification of ancient Jewish law that gives standards of behavior and reflects an attitude obviously inherited from that culture's Old Testament roots. And the *Mishnah* has much to say regarding the duties of a married woman.

As part of her household work, a wife was to grind flour, bake, launder, cook, nurse her children, make the beds, spin wool, prepare the children for school, and take them to school to assure their arrival. Instruction for the children, however, took place primarily in the home. A rabbi could take no money for his teaching, unless he was asked to teach children, since he was doing what parents were required to do.

What about any other employment? We know from the *Mishnah* that some women did work together with their husbands in the fields picking fruit, but it was usually alongside of and in support of their husbands. The *Mishnah* does tell us there were women who worked in the marketplace apart from their husbands, but there were those who considered such activity a disgrace to the society. The wife might also do crafts or horticulture at home and sell the fruits of her labor. That provided a supplement to the husband's income or was kept as pocket money for her own use. And although a housewife was kept very busy with her work in the home, she was still expected to dress and adorn herself properly, as stressed in many of the traditions.

In addition, apart from her household work, the *Mishnah* indicates that the wife was also responsible for hospitality and the care of guests. Wives were active in charitable work: they gave alms to the poor who came to their homes and participated in charitable projects outside the home. The *Mishnah* elevates and honors the woman's position in the home. The Jewish standards were very clear:

the woman's priority was in the home. Beyond her family, she was to take care of the needs of strangers, the poor, and any guests who might come along. Then, she could work alongside her husband, and if she had any time or energy left she could be enterprising in other ways.

TODAY'S WOMAN AND THE TEACHING OF GOD'S WORD

The Jewish tradition fit, generally, the biblical model. Today's generation of women, however, is far from that biblical and traditional model. And it is sad to consider what the next generation of mothers will be like if biblical priorities aren't regained and preserved.

One of the most unfortunate results of today's generation of working mothers is that the mother's instruction and influence on the children is lost. Biblically, the responsibility to raise children rests with the home. Proverbs 1:8-9 says a child is to listen not only to his father's instruction but also to the law of his *mother*. She needs to build up her own spiritual life so that she can be a godly mother to her children: available in a crisis, ready to teach them. Times of teaching often require preparation, and that is a priority. I don't believe that God expects a mother to go out and work full time just so she can send her children to a Christian school, expecting the Christian school to overcome the lack of commitment and availability on her part. She must be preoccupied with the task of spiritual instruction, committed to teaching her children the things of God.

When a wife has fulfilled her God-given priorities in the family, she has a responsibility to reach beyond to help the poor and needy, to be involved in ministering to nonfamily people. Women who are home during the day should be a valuable resource to people in their community. Until all of those priorities are fulfilled, a woman has no right to pursue other activities, however enterprising and creative they may be.

We need to ask an important question at this point. If the home is God's ordained priority for women, why is there so much rebellion? A return to Genesis will explain it. Genesis 1:27-28 says, "And God created man in His own image, in the image of God He created them; male and female He created them. And God blessed them; and God said to *them*, 'Be fruitful and multiply, and fill the earth, and subdue it; and rule . . .' " (italics added). Notice that when God first made them, even though He made the woman to be a suitable helper (Genesis 2:18), and even though He made the man to be the head (1 Corinthians 11:3-9; 1 Timothy 2:11-14), God said to *them* "Be fruitful and multiply . . . fill the earth . . . subdue it . . . and rule." They were co-regents: they ruled together. Headship and submission were so wonderfully blended in perfect harmony that they are not even visible in the perfect oneness prior to the Fall. Adam and Eve multiplied *together*, filled and subdued the earth *together*, and ruled *together*.

But in Genesis 3 sin entered the picture, and immediately they were cursed. Consider the elements of the curse for the woman, in verse 16: "To the woman He said, I will greatly multiply your pain in childbirth, in pain you shall bring forth children." The pain of childbirth was to be a constant reminder to every woman that she is a victim of sin. But that is only part of the curse. "Yet your desire shall be for your husband, and he shall rule over you." Most commentators say that "your desire" simply refers to the normal strong sexual and psychological attraction a woman has for her husband, and the normal function of the husband to rule over his wife. But in most cases the truth is that a man has a much stronger desire for sexual fulfillment than does a woman. That fact contradicts the traditional interpretation. Also, historically women have not loved their role of submission to their husbands. There isn't a period in history when women haven't chafed under male authority. One more thing: if this were simply a normal desire it would not involve a curse. Whatever verse 16 means, it has to be something different now from what it was before the Fall.

The key to understanding this passage is the word translated "rule," which is *masal* in Hebrew. In the Septuagint the word used is *kathistēmi*, which means "to install in an office" or "to elevate to an official position." So as part of the curse God said to the woman, "You were once co-regents, you ruled together as a team, but from now on the man is installed over you." This is a new kind of ruling that had not been known before. The man's authority was never intended to be despotic, but in the Fall it became just that. Eve usurped the headship of her husband when she took the fruit—and fell into sin. The curse on her is that the man is going to have to rule over her for the rest of human history. But that's only part of the picture.

The rest is found in the latter part of verse 16: "Yet your desire shall be for your husband." The word translated "desire" is used only one other time in the Pentateuch, in Genesis 4:7. It comes from an Arabic root that means "to compel, to impel, to urge, to seek control." In Genesis 4:7, God is speaking to Cain: "[Sin's] desire is for you, but you must master it." In other words, sin will desire to *control* or to *master* Cain. It is the same word that appears in Genesis 3:16, in the identical form, in the same grammatical structure. So whatever it means in 4:7 it would also mean back in 3:16, because it is in the same context. So Genesis 3:16 would rightly read: "To the woman He said . . . Your desire shall be to *control* your husband, but he shall rule over you." Adam would subdue Eve's tendency to control him. And because Adam followed her lead in sinning willfully (3:17), God adds to the curse and says to men, in effect, "From now on women will seek to control men." That is the curse. And therein lies the battle of the sexes. Women trying to rule (women's liberation) and men trying to crush the revolt (male chauvinism).

Is there an answer to the curse of this struggle between men and women? Yes! *In Jesus Christ the curse may be erased!* Women have been oppressed by the crushing power of men who want to keep them subdued. And men have been harassed by women who want to rise to the top and take over, but Christians have the answer—Jesus Christ. When He comes into a life and the Holy Spirit of God fills it, men and women submit to the God-ordained pattern and the home becomes like it was in the garden before the Fall: *together* they're fruitful, *together* they multiply, *together* they have dominion, and *together* they work out God's plan in their lives. Wives willingly submit and husbands lovingly lead.

THE NEW TESTAMENT TEACHING REGARDING WIDOWS

The argument of necessity is often used to justify women's working outside the home. *Someone* has to provide income, and in cases where there is no father, who is to do it if not the mother?

Such reasoning may seem logical but in light of biblical teaching it breaks down. In homes with no father, the mother's presence is more necessary than ever. I believe the answer in such situations lies in the New Testament teaching regarding widows.

First Timothy 5:3-16 summarizes Paul's teaching on widows. Verse 3 says: "Honor widows who are widows indeed." Widows without resources ("widows indeed") are to be cared for and supported ("honor" means "pay" here, cf. v. 17), and not forced to go to work, again reinforcing that a woman's primary ministry is in the home. I believe this principle of supporting a woman without resources could even be applied, for example, to a believing wife whose unbelieving husband divorces or abandons her, leaving her with children at home. She should not be forced to go to work, further robbing the children. The sum is that a woman who has no resources is to be given what she needs for support.

You say, "Who is to take care of this responsibility?" Notice verse 4: "But if any widow has children or grandchildren [I think these are men in view here], let them first learn to practice piety [at home], and to make some return to their parents; for this is acceptable in the sight of God." If a man is so related to a widow without resources, he is to demonstrate his holiness in the home by supplying her needs *before* demonstrating it in the church. Again, this is so that she may remain in the ministry of the home, to fulfill the divine priority. And in so doing, the principle of man as provider and protector of woman is reinforced.

So what is a woman to do when she becomes a "widow indeed"? Is she to begin by checking out the job ads? No. "Now she who is a widow indeed, and who has been left alone has fixed her hope on God, and continues in entreaties and prayers night and day" (v. 5). In other words, she is to fall on her knees and beseech God for the supply of her need. She is to cast herself on God's mercy. That is the reason the Bible so pointedly instructs us regarding meeting the needs of widows. James calls it "pure and undefiled religion" to help the fatherless and widows (James 1:27). This is the responsibility of the people of God—and it always has been.

A negative alternative to the widow's seeking God is given in verse 6: "But she who gives herself to wanton pleasure is dead even while she lives."

The widow who falls into a pleasure-mad life is as dead as her husband. Why? Because she is deadening herself to God's standards. There are only two choices here. Either she is on her knees praying or she is out in the world, exposing herself to its evil. This passage doesn't suggest finding a job as an alternative. The widow is to be cared for. And verse 7 says that these things are to be commanded. These principles are not options or thoughts to ponder. They are commands, and to disobey them is to be guilty.

Then Paul says a word directly to the men who bear the task of support. "But if any one does not provide for his own, and especially for those of his household, he has denied the faith, and is worse than an unbeliever" (v. 8). This is a serious matter. Men need to support those widows who are related to them, if those women have no resources, rather than forcing them out to work. That is God's standard, and not to do it is to deny the faith. Also, not to support widows would be to do less than many unbelievers.

Someone might ask, "What if there are no men in the family to support a widow?" According to verse 16, if there is no man who can fulfill this responsibility, a believing woman can step in: "If any woman who is a believer has dependent widows, let her assist them." Those women who have the resources could minister to a widow by providing her with a place to stay, clothing, and so on. But what about the widow who has no family members to care for her, men or women? The last part of verse 16 speaks to that: "Let not the church be burdened, so that it may assist those who are widows indeed." If there is no one to meet the need, the church is called to do it. And that does not necessarily mean the organized church must include it in the budget. It means that the *people* who make up the community of faith are to reach out to that widow in her need, whether corporately or individually.

The point to make in all this is that a woman is to be cared for, not left to her own resources—especially when there is no father or other man in the family. She is to fix her hope on God, who then commands first the men, then the women, and finally the church: "Gather that widow in your arms." And by the way, that is precisely what the early church did (Acts 2:44-45; 4:32-36; 6:1-6).

Verse 9 refers to the care of widows by the church: "Let a widow be put on the list only if she is not less than sixty years old." The phrase "put on the list" refers to a "widow's list" kept by the early church. That list involved two things: (1) The church took on her support when she reached the age of sixty; (2) such widows constituted an official group who represented the church in ministry—"staff widows," if you will.

There were other prerequisites to being put on the list. The first one is at the end of verse 9: "Having been the wife of one man." The Greek indicates not an outward fact, but an inward attitude, a one-man woman, devoted and loving to her own husband. Paul is not forbidding a woman who had a divorce or former marriage. The idea is the intensity of her commitment to the man who was her husband. She was to be a woman who *loved* her husband. As Paul says of the wife in 1 Corinthians

7:34, she lives "to please her husband."

Further, she must have "a reputation for good works" (v. 10*a*). What were some of these good works? "If she has brought up children [not just *bore* children, but brought them up]." Also, "if she has shown hospitality to strangers." She had to be available to be hospitable, to have a home where there was always food, a warm reception, and a bed for someone who needed it. She also had to have "washed the saints' feet . . . assisted those in distress, and . . . devoted herself to every good work." To meet all of those requirements a woman *had* to be at home!

Paul sums up his teaching in verses 11-15 by saying basically, "Don't put the younger widows on the list." Why? Because it would be very hard for them to keep their original commitment as a mature widow could. They might begin their ministry in total devotion and service to Christ, but after a period of time feel the desire to be married again, which was their right to do. So they might throw off their original commitment, "thus incurring condemnation" (v. 12). This verse is not talking about them losing their salvation, but refers to the chastening due for breaking their pledge to be solely devoted to Christ.

The danger is that once such a young widow turns from that total commitment to Christ, to desiring a husband, the church's financial support, instead of enabling her to maintain a godly lifestyle, would allow her the leisure to "learn to be idle as they go around from house to house; and not merely idle, but also gossips and busybodies, talking about things not proper to mention. There-fore I want younger widows to get married, bear children, keep house, and give the enemy no occa-sion for reproach; for some have already turned aside to follow Satan" (vv. 13-15). In other words, a younger widow was to be remarried and return to the home with a husband who would take care of her. She was to bear children and be a keeper at home. And again, there is that divine priority.

And that is the only biblical priority—that wives be committed to their homes and to their hus-bands. It is a high calling, a holy responsibility. It is exalting, not degrading, to the submissive woman.

Christianity does not offer to the world a sup-pression of women or an exaltation of men, or vice versa. God offers, through Jesus Christ and the power of the indwelling Holy Spirit, the perfection of men and women in their divinely ordained and created intention. And when that happens, when the home becomes the place where spiritual life functions, God will raise up a holy generation and perpetuate it into the next one. And that is the only hope of the world. It is also the only way to experi-ence God's blessing.

A woman's priorities are given by the One who created woman. He knows the way to fulfillment. And there is no true joy apart from obedience to these priorities.

QUESTIONS FOR DISCUSSION

1. How did the teachings of Jewish law describe the duties of the wife?

2. Modern society has introduced a variety of roles for women. Can these be reconciled with the biblical model?

3. What were the roles of Adam and Eve before the Fall? How were their roles changed after the Fall?

4. What does the Bible say about caring for widows? Who is responsible for their care? When should the church support a widow?

5. If a woman becomes a widow, what are her options (1 Timothy 5:5-6)?

Part Three

God's Pattern for Husbands

Husbands, love your wives, just as Christ also loved the church and gave Himself up for her; that He might sanctify her, having cleansed her by the washing of water with the word, that He might present to Himself the church in all her glory, having no spot or wrinkle or any such thing; but that she should be holy and blameless. So husbands ought also to love their own wives as their own bodies. He who loves his own wife loves himself; for no one ever hated his own flesh, but nourishes and cherishes it, just as Christ also does the church, because we are members of His body. For this cause a man shall leave his father and mother, and shall cleave to his wife; and the two shall become one flesh. This mystery is great; but I am speaking with reference to Christ and the church. Nevertheless let each individual among you also love his own wife even as himself; and let the wife see to it that she respect her husband.

—Ephesians 5:25-33

4

An All-Out Attack on Marriage

The great English war hero Field Marshal Montgomery once said to his young troops: "Gentlemen, don't even think about marriage until you have mastered the art of warfare!" You may be thinking, *I can relate to that!* Why is marriage such a potential warfare? Why does it seem to be so hard to have a dynamic love relationship with another person? One of the most promising relationships is that which occurs between a man and a woman in marriage, yet the fulfillment of it can be so elusive. Having a significant, lasting relationship with someone, a union that gets better, richer, and more fulfilling, is becoming increasingly rare. In fact, marriage is usually portrayed as a fighting, unfaithful, discontended, bitter relationship ending in separation or divorce. And there are some reasons for that.

THE CURSE OF GOD

We return to the early chapters of Genesis to find the origin of marital problems. In Genesis

2:18 God said, "It is not good for the man to be alone; I will make him a helper suitable for him." Then verse 19 describes the creation of the animal world and the naming of all the animals by Adam. Verse 20 points out: "And the man gave names to all the cattle, and to the birds of the sky, and to every beast of the field, but for Adam there was not found a helper suitable for him." So in verses 21-22 God provided this helper to aid Adam as he ruled creation. Notice that from the very beginning God designed someone to be in charge and someone to help: someone to be in authority and someone to submit to that authority: someone to be the provider, and someone for whom to provide. From the beginning the man had the place of headship and the woman was the one for whom that headship was provided.

Adam first acknowledged his wife in verse 23 by saying: "This is now bone of my bones and flesh of my flesh; she shall be called Woman, because she was taken out of Man." God adds the postscript in verse 24: "For this cause a man shall leave his father and his mother, and shall cleave to his wife; and they shall become one flesh." It was a marvelous, perfect relationship. Adam viewed Eve in every sense as one with him—that was God's design. He was the leader and she was to follow his lead, but in such perfect balance that the roles were really lost within their oneness. The woman's submissiveness and the man's provision were both willing and beautiful. There was no animosity, no struggle, no conflict—only a glorious union.

God's purposes for marriage are really very simple. First, marriage is for the propagation of the race (Genesis 1:27). Second, it is designed to eliminate solitude and loneliness (Genesis 2:18). Third, Paul indicates in 1 Corinthians 7:2 that God has ordained marriage as a deterrent to immorality. Finally, God wants marriage to be a relationship of pure enjoyment in which the partners know the thrill of a satisfying physical relationship (Hebrews 13:4). So God made marriage a beautifully unique relationship in which the woman as the helper is to joyfully support the man, and he as the head is to joyfully love the woman.

But something monumental occurred in the record of Genesis 3. The serpent bypassed the headship of the man and went to the one who was by nature the follower. He enticed the woman to do the one thing God had told them not to do—eat of the fruit of the tree of the knowledge of good and evil (Genesis 2:17). She took the fruit, ate it, and gave it to her husband, and he took it and ate. Here we see the reversal of their roles. The woman usurped the leadership of the man, and the man became the follower. God's design for marriage was twisted at that moment of temptation, and the legacy has been the defilement of marriage relations. Because there has been since that one act a reversal of the roles as God had designed them, marriage faces great difficulty. In fact, in the curse of Genesis 3:16-19 we find that the most basic elements of human life are involved:

Child-bearing (v. 16*a*). The wonderful anticipation, joy, and hope in having a child will be somewhat overshadowed by the physical pain and anguish of childbirth.

Marriage (v. 16*b*). There will now be a problem in marriage because the man is going to rule over the woman in an oppressive way, and the woman will seek to rule over the man.

Provision (vv. 17-19). Man will have to labor and sweat to earn a living and provide for his family.

Life (2:17). God had said to Adam concerning the forbidden tree: "In the day that you eat from it you shall surely die." Spiritual and even physical death are a result of the sin in the garden. And when Adam sinned, his death and his sin "spread to all men," (Romans 5:12). The race itself was cursed.

When we look at human society today we cannot deny death or the pain of childbirth or the difficulty of earning a living: and we must also admit that the cause of conflict in marriage is the total reversal of marital roles that came about in Adam and Eve's sin at the beginning. Women's liberation and male chauvinism are simply manifestations of depravity, fallenness, and the curse.

So at least two things are needful to have a marriage that works: (1) a woman characterized by submission, that beautiful humility woman knew before the Fall; and (2) a man characterized by sacrificial love, whose commitment is to love his wife and provide for her everything he would for himself—as was true before the Fall. Two sinful people, whose depravity will inevitably manifest itself, make this a task possible only through clear understanding and divine power. Husbands find it hard to love their wives because it isn't natural. It's natural to love ourselves, to be self-consumed, self-preoccupied, and self-absorbed. As long as a person is like that he is not able to give himself in love to someone else.

Men in our society are no different from men in the past—they suppress women, they crush them down, they turn them into sex objects. Why? Because that is the legacy of sin! But it doesn't have to be that way. It is possible to have a right relationship in which a woman is lifted up, exalted, and allowed to be all that God ever intended her to be; and in which the man knows how to invest his life in lovingly providing for her, thus reestablishing that coregency that fulfills every need of the human heart.

THE CORRUPTION BY SATAN

It would be bad enough that marriage operates under the divine curse, but the attack does not end there. Satan takes his shots at marriage, too. As soon as sin entered the world, Satan began to attack marriage. He tried to crush marriage because he knew it was the foundation of right human relations. His effort is to devastate the world by destroying relationships at their most important level—the home. So Genesis records that after the Fall, Satan systematically tried to corrupt God's design for marriage and family life by polygamy (4:19, 23), evil sexual thoughts and words (9:22), adultery (16:1-3), homosexuality (19:4-11), fornication and rape (34:1-2), incest (38:13-18), prostitution (38:24), and evil seduction (39:7-12). So fallen human nature, the curse on the physical world, and the attack of hell's hosts all amass their guns to destroy marriage and the home. Trying to make marriage work without God's power is impossible.

Is it becoming clearer why marriage is so tough, why there are so many divorces, so many miserable people, so many unhappy relationships? Do you see why you struggle?

THE CONFUSION OF SOCIETY

As if the elements of the curse and the corruption of Satan aren't enough to make marriage difficult, add to them a society that applauds evil as if it were virtuous. Television, movies, magazines, books, and music all mock the design of God, making it hard to live a godly life in the home. The only people who can pull it off are people who (1) know the Lord Jesus Christ (Ephesians 1-3), and (2) are filled with His Spirit (Ephesians 5:18). Apart from those requirements a person has no more hope of making marriage work the way God designed it than Ponce de Leon had of finding the fountain of youth. It simply will not happen by itself. If you can't make marriage work, everything else is miserable. The curse hit us at the heart of one of life's greatest needs. "It is not good for the man to be alone." Man desperately desires a helper, so Satan smashes him at the very base of his profoundest need. And then along comes this sick world system, spawned by Satan himself, and it tells us that if we really want to live it up we should be unfaithful, have an affair here and there, swap wives, and so on. The confusion gets worse and worse and fulfilling relationships become almost impossible to find.

Our society, frustrated with the reality, throws down a fantasy in front of itself. Just think about some of the songs we hear. They sing about the perfect woman or the perfect man, the dreamed-of perfect relationship, where there won't be any boredom or unfaithfulness, no breakup, no pain or loneliness. But it is all a pipe dream! A new partnership is fast turned from a dream to the same old reality. People looking for something special don't know where to find it, so, sadly, they settle for illusions and fantasies. Add to that an overwhelming preoccupation with the physical in fashion and figure, and the onslaught is like the legions of Rome marching on a small village.

GOD'S CURE FOR THE PROBLEMS OF MARRIAGE CONFLICT

Ephesians 5:22-23 is crucially important, if we are to understand how marriage works. It is the greatest treatise on marriage ever written. Here is marriage as it was before the Fall, and as it *can be again.* If we are ever to see the divine and joyous ideal in our marriages, Christ must be at their center and the Spirit of God must pervade them. Once a married couple is "in Christ" (Ephesians 1-3) and "filled with the Spirit" (Ephesians 5:18), it becomes possible for the wife to submit to her husband and the husband to love his wife. Christian marriage, as God designed it and as Paul discusses it here in Ephesians 5, *is a reversal of the Fall.* The ultimate tragedy is conflict in a Christian marriage, because it denies all the potential that God has placed in that union. If you are a Christian you have all the resources necessary to realize fully the potential beauty and joy God built into your marriage.

Now we turn to an examination of the husband as God has designed him to be. His role is broadly and clearly defined. I will introduce it in this chapter and give the details in the next.

THE DUTY OF THE HUSBAND

Paul's instruction to husbands is summed up in the opening phrase of Ephesians 5:25: "Husbands, love your wives." The husband submits to his wife in the spirit of verse 21 by loving her.

The word Paul uses here for "love" is *agapaō*, the strongest, most intimate, most far-reaching, and most qualitative term for love. Yes, there is to be authority in a marriage. Yes, there is one who is the head and one who follows. But verse 25 does not say, "Husbands, *rule* your wives," or, "Husbands, *subject* your wives," or, "Husbands, *command* your wives." No! Paul says, "Husbands, *love* your wives."

How is a husband to demonstrate his love to his wife? In verse 25 the apostle gives us the supreme model of the manner in which a husband should love his wife: "As Christ also loved the church."

How did Christ love His church? Look at Romans 5:8: "But God demonstrates His own love toward us, in that while we were yet sinners, Christ died for us." How did Christ love the church? He gave the greatest gift for the most unworthy people. He is absolutely holy and righteous, untainted and unspotted by sin. Yet this perfect One made the ultimate sacrifice for the worst of sinners. *That* is how He loved the church!

People seeking to end a marriage often say, "I can't forgive my partner anymore. He or she has done too many things, gone too far." But that is not the standard here, is it? An absolutely righteous God made the greatest act of sacrifice for the vilest of people. Husbands can never offer Christ any excuses about wives' problems causing them to lose their love. Your wife may be a sinner, but so are you. And Christ loves you just the same. Don't lose that perspective. A husband may say, "I have decided I don't love her anymore." If that is true, that husband is disobedient to the command of God, for God commands husbands to love their wives.

Romans 8:35-39 tells us even more about the love of Christ: "Who shall separate us from the love of Christ? Shall tribulation, or distress, or persecution, or famine, or nakedness, or peril, or sword?" Notice verses 38 and 39: "For I am convinced that neither death, nor life, nor angels, nor principalities, nor things present, nor things to come, nor powers, nor height, nor depth, nor any other created thing, shall be able to separate us from the love of God, which is in Christ Jesus our

Lord." Husbands, there is nothing that can separate us from His love, and we are to love our wives like Christ loves His church. Loving is an act of the will. If you determine you're not going to do it, you won't: but if you determine you're going to do it by the grace of God, in spite of whatever happens, as Jesus loves the church, no matter what comes you will love her.

Let me suggest three very practical ways to express that love:

Consideration. First Peter 3:7 says: "You husbands likewise, live with your wives in an understanding way." To love her demands sensitivity, understanding, and consideration. Women often complain about their husbands, "He never understands me, he's insensitive to my needs, we never talk, he doesn't know how I feel." Lack of consideration often builds a wall in a marriage. Peter tells us to tear it down. He says, in essence, "Be sensitive, be understanding, feel what she feels."

Chivalry. Peter continues in verse 7: "As with a weaker vessel, since she is a woman." In other words, men need to remember that physically they are stronger than women. Do you practice courtesy and thoughtfulness, such as opening the car door for your wife? Or are you fifteen feet out the driveway while she still has one foot hanging out the door? Remember, your wife is the weaker vessel.

Communion. Peter reminds us at the end of the seventh verse: "Grant her honor as a fellow-heir of the grace of life, so that your prayers may not be hindered." This phrase "the grace of life" means marriage is like the hot fudge on a hot fudge sundae. Marriage is the topping, the best part of life. And since you've inherited marriage, fulfill it together, will you? Commune together, talk together, share together. I thank the Lord for my wife. She's my best friend, my closest confidante. We commune together. And there is a key spiritual thought here too—"so that your prayers may not be hindered." A wrong marriage relation closes the windows of heaven.

So God has given us the ingredients to make marriage thrilling, productive, and blessed. The curse can be reversed when two people are in Christ and filled with His Spirit. Particularly when we husbands determine in our hearts that we are going to love our wives as Christ loved the church; and that we will make whatever sacrifice is necessary for them; and that we will be considerate, be chivalrous, and commune with them on a spiritual level; then marriage will become everything God ever meant it to be. When that happens you will be giving a legacy to your children that will affect not only their marriages but those of generations to come.

QUESTIONS FOR DISCUSSION

1. What elements of human life are included in the curses of sin (Genesis 3:16-19)? How do they affect us?

2. Why does Satan want to destroy marriages? How does he use fallen human nature to do it?

3. What is God's cure for conflict in marriage (Ephesians 5:22-23)? How is it possible to achieve this?

4. What is the husband's primary duty to his wife?

5 What model is the husband given for demonstrating love to his wife (Ephesians 5:25)?

6. What are some practical ways for husbands to express love to their wives?

5

Husbands, Love Your Wives

Some years ago *The Saturday Evening Post* carried an article entitled "The Seven Ages of the Married Cold." It revealed the reactions of a husband to his wife's colds during their first seven years of marriage. It went something like this:

The first year. "Sugar dumpling, I'm really worried about my baby girl. You've got a bad sniffle and there's no telling about these things with all this strep going around. I'm putting you in the hospital this afternoon for a general checkup and a good rest. I know the food's lousy, but I'll be bringing your meals in from Rossini's. I've already got it all arranged with the floor superintendent."

The second year. "Listen darling, I don't like the sound of that cough. I've called Doc Miller and asked him to rush over here. Now you go to bed like a good girl, please, just for papa."

The third year. "Maybe you'd better lie down, honey: nothing like a rest when you feel lousy.

I'll bring you something. Have you got any canned soup?"

The fourth year. "Now look, dear, be sensible. After you've fed the kids, washed the dishes, and finished the floors, you'd better lie down."

The fifth year. "Why don't you take a couple of aspirin?"

The sixth year. "I wish you would just gargle or something instead of sitting around all evening barking like a seal."

The seventh year. "For Pete's sake, stop sneezing! Are you trying to give me pneumonia?"

The decline of marriage, as seen through the common cold! A humorous look at a not-so-humorous reality.

Dr. Carl Rogers, in his book *Becoming Partners: Marriage and Its Alternatives* (Delta Books, 1973), said:

> To me it seems that we are living in an important and uncertain age, and the institution of marriage is most assuredly in an uncertain state. If 50-75 percent of Ford or General Motors cars completely fell apart within the early part of their lifetimes as automobiles, drastic steps would be taken. We have no such well-organized way of dealing with our social institutions, so people are groping, more or less blindly, to find alternatives to marriage (which is certainly less than 50 percent successful). Living together without marriage, living in communes, extensive child care centers, serial monogomy (one divorce after another), the women's liberation movement to establish the woman as a person in her own right, new divorce laws which do away with the concept of guilt—these are all gropings toward some new form of man-

woman relationship for the future. It would take a bolder man than I to predict what will emerge.

How curious that Rogers admits that the alternatives to marriage are gropings for a new definition of man-woman relationships! But there is no need to grope: what is needful is to go back to the Creator to discover how these relationships ought to work. And that brings us back to what the Bible says. Rogers said it would take a bolder man than him to predict what will happen to marriage. God's Word has the answer to that challenge, in 2 Timothy 3.

Second Timothy 3:1 says: "But realize this, that in the last days difficult times will come." Then in verse 13, which is a summary of those difficult times, Paul writes: "Evil men and impostors will proceed from bad to worse, deceiving and being deceived." Things are going to get worse, not better. And to define the character of those evil days we need to consider verse 2: "For men will be lovers of self." We will see in the last days an overwhelming amount of self-centeredness, selfishness, self-absorption, self-indulgence, and self-satisfaction. People will be looking only for self-satisfaction. They will fall more and more in love with themselves. Ego has always been the greatest problem, so the society of the last days just stops fighting it, adopts pride as a virtue, and commends it.

Another characteristic of the last days is that children will be "disobedient to parents" (v. 2*b*). Children will lose respect for their parents' authority, there will be rebellion in the family with a corresponding lack of obedience to parents. We see it already in epidemic proportions. And with all of the chaos in families some children never even comprehend what a parent's place is, so disobedience is an obvious result.

Another interesting characteristic of the people of the last days recorded in verse 3*a* is "unloving." The Greek word is *astorgoi*, which is from *storgē*, meaning "family affection." When you add the *a* in front of it the word means literally "without family affection." In other words, we can expect the last times to be characterized by self-love, rebellion in the family, and lack of normal family love. When that happens, the home turns into something perverted. In the last days, everything will come crashing down on the home, God's basic unit of human society and righteous heritage. That is the apostle's message in this prophetic passage.

So in chapter 4 we saw that meaningful marriage is difficult because of the curse of God, the corruption of Satan, and the confusion of society. Now add to these the characteristics of the last days and it becomes apparent that there is little hope for marriage, at least on human terms. But there *is* a way marriage may produce relationships that are designed and fulfilled the way God intended them. We are affirming that as we study Ephesians 5.

THE MANNER OF LOVE

We have already indicated that the husband is first and always to love his wife. Let's look deeper into the manner in which husbands are to love and lead their wives: "As Christ also loved the church." The standard is infinitely high, isn't it? Of course, Paul is talking not about the fullness of the capacity of divine love, but about the *kind* of love that Christ manifested. Obviously we cannot love to the extent that He did, but we can have the same type of love for our wives. So we need to ask how Christ loved the church. There are at least four qualities of that love.

Sacrificial love (v. 25). First of all Christ's love was a sacrificial love. He "gave Himself up" for us. Jesus Christ loved the church in eternity past enough to leave heaven, come to earth, take on a human form, suffer through humanness and rejection, be spit on and mocked, be crowned with a crown of thorns, be nailed to a cross, and have a spear drilled into His side. He loved the church enough to *die*. Such sacrificial love is to mark the love of a husband for his wife. When Christ gave up His prerogative to be in eternity with God and chose to come to earth in the form of a servant, He was acting in sacrificial love.

Keep in mind that this kind of love can never be deserved. When God by His infinite, sovereign love placed people in the Body of Christ, when they were chosen to be His children, it was not because they were deserving! Sacrificial love is unmerited love. God is not rescuing people who deserve it, He is rescuing people who *don't* deserve it, just because it is His nature to love. A love which gives only to those who earn the right to receive it is an inferior kind of love. It may not be love at all, because no sacrifice or self-giving is involved.

The world usually thinks like that. If the object of their love is nice, the world says, "I love you." People choose to love others who live up to their expectations or fit into their group. The world's kind of love is object-oriented, but God's love is very different. God does not focus on the object: it is His nature to love. That is the difference. God just loves, *period*. God was not externally bound to love this unattractive world. The world hated Him, but God loved the world. It is not the *object* that calls forth the love of God; it is His *nature* to love.

So when Paul tells husbands to love their wives he is not saying, "Love her because she deserves it." We are commanded to love our wives: that is the issue, not the attractiveness or worthiness of the object. I have also discovered, however, that what you *choose* to love will become greatly attractive to you. A heart determined to love sees only beauty.

Even though sacrificial love is undeserved, it reaches to the greatest lengths, as exemplified in Christ. It says, "You may not deserve anything, but I give you everything. I would even die for you!" And Paul is saying that that is the attitude a husband is to have toward his wife. He must come to the place where he can say to her, "I will love you, commit myself to you, and give you everything I have. I will even die for you!" *That's* the issue. And such love is not resignation, but the expression of an eager, joyful heart.

Let me hasten to add that love, as God defines it,

is not an emotion or a feeling. But the world says, "When the feeling stops, your love is over, so walk away." That is not the love of which the Bible speaks. Biblical love is not some "goose bump" but an act of selfless sacrifice, and whoever has need is worthy of it.

In John 13, Jesus' disciples were in the upper room arguing about which of them would be the greatest in the kingdom. They were on an ego trip: they were being selfish, self-centered, self-indulgent, and insensitive to Jesus and the pain and sin He was about to bear. In their self-indulgence they wouldn't wash each others' feet. Finally, Jesus knelt down and washed their filthy feet, and when He finished He said, "A new commandment I give you, that you love one another, even as I have loved you" (v. 34). And how had He loved them? Not by feeling emotional! But He washed their feet anyway, because love does not do what it *feels*, it does what is *needed*. Where there is a need, love acts, sacrificially. And that is the husband's part in marriage.

Husbands, you will never really know how to love until you've sacrificed yourself, crucified yourself, and died to yourself. Paul says true love "does not seek its own" (1 Corinthians 13:5). As long as a man is looking for what can be personally gained from marriage he will never know what it is to love his wife as Christ loved the church, and he can never experience the richness of self-giving and its amazing dividends.

Ask yourself a question: when was the last time you made a sacrifice for your wife? When was the last time you wanted to do different things and you said, "Honey, I'm ready to do what you want to do." Sometimes we need to lay aside our carefully made plans and do what she thinks we ought to do. The issue is sacrificial love. And husbands must die to themselves to have that kind of love. Our world tells us just the opposite: "Be the macho man, the big shot. Don't let anyone step on your territory, fight back, grab for all you can get because you deserve it." But the Bible simply says, "Set yourself aside." Somewhere along the line if you are to love that woman in your house like Christ loved the church, you will have to see the death of your own selfish desires.

Purifying love (vv. 26-27). The love a man is to have for his wife is also to be a purifying love. Jesus gave Himself for the church so that "He might sanctify her, having cleansed her by the washing of water with the word, that He might present to Himself the church in all her glory, having no spot or wrinkle or any such thing; but that she should be holy and blameless." We learn from this a very basic truth: when a man loves someone, that person's purity is his supreme concern. No one loves and wants to defile whom they love. Christ loved His church, so He wanted to purify His people. When someone is saved, the Lord Jesus Christ cleanses every sin he has ever committed, or will commit. The moment we open our hearts and invite Jesus Christ in, He cleanses us absolutely so that "though your sins are as scarlet, they will be as white as snow" (Isaiah 1:18). He has removed our sin as far as the east is from the west

(Psalm 103:12*a*), He has buried it in the depths of the deepest sea and remembers it against us no more (Micah 7:19; Jeremiah 31:34). We are clean through the blood of Christ. His love does all that.

In John 13:10 Jesus said to Peter, "He who has bathed needs only to wash his feet." Jesus used the Greek word *luō* for the idea of a complete bath. In the Orient a person would bathe himself in the morning. Then as he went through the day he would just have to wash *(niptō)* his feet. When we came to Christ we were cleansed positionally before God. That settled our eternal destiny. But every day as we walk through the world our feet get dusty and we need the daily washing Jesus speaks of here. That deals with our fellowship. When we were saved all our sins were washed away, yet 1 John 1:19 says that Jesus keeps on cleansing us from all sin. We were bathed once, and now we're kept continuously pure, so that our communion might be full and rich.

Marriage also involves a purification. A man takes his partner out of the world and apart from the past. Marriage sets two people apart unto each other and in that sense purifies them. And if a man really loves his wife he seeks that which keeps her feet clean from the dust of the world, doing everything in his power to maintain her holiness, her virtue, and her purity. Love always seeks to purify! He would never do anything that would lead her or provoke her to sin.

Go back to verse 26. Christ sanctifies and cleanses the church "by the washing of water with the word." It is the Word of God that keeps us pure (cf. John 15:3). God's Word redeemed us, and God's Word keeps us clean. Husbands have the responsibility in the home to provide for the wives every purifying influence that will make them holy. That means they are to teach them the cleansing Word. A wife is a man's first priority for ministry.

In verse 27, Paul says that the Lord wants to present to Himself the church "in all her glory" (*endoxon*, "an intense splendidness"), not having any stain or flaw, but absolutely holy and without a blemish. That is how a man must deal with his wife—never doing anything that would lead her into any illicit thought or relationship, never doing anything that would cause her to look to someone else for fulfillment. Fulfilling his love to her so that she is purified, sanctified, and lifted to God—that is a husband's responsibility.

Caring love (vv. 28-30). Marriage should also evidence a caring love. Paul says in verse 28: "So husbands ought also to love their own wives as their own bodies. He who loves his own wife loves himself." We spend a lot of time on our own bodies—exercising, eating the right food, wearing nice clothes, and so on. We take care of ourselves, and we ought to, because the Christian's body is the temple of the Holy Spirit. So Paul says, "You ought to love your wives like you love your own bodies." Again, notice that love is not an emotion. When our bodies have needs we meet them. Our wives have needs too, and we are God's agents to meet them. And even though love is not an emotion, I believe that joyful emotion will follow such meeting of a need.

Verse 29 adds to the thought: "For no one ever hated his own flesh, but nourishes and cherishes it, just as Christ also does the church." Does the Lord care for the church? Does He supply everything we need? Philippians 4:19 says He does: "My God shall supply all your needs according to His riches in glory in Christ Jesus." If you need love, joy, peace, strength, wisdom, or anything else, He promises to give it to you. And God is telling husbands to supply everything their wives need. Don't forget, the man is the provider, the protector, and the preserver. We are to care for our wives like we care for our own bodies, like Christ cares for the church!

That word *nourish* is a marvelous word, *ektrephō*, which means "to nourish, to feed." Primarily, it was used in reference to nurturing or bringing up children. It basically means "to mature." Husbands are called to nurture their wives, to help bring them to maturity. Also, because *ektrephō* literally means "to feed," I believe this reinforces the principle that the man is to be the breadwinner, the provider. What did you provide for your salvation? Nothing. What resources do you provide to live the Christian life? None. As Christ provides all for the church, so does a husband provide all for his wife. That is the biblical pattern. Husbands are to nourish, feed, and cause their wives to mature spiritually.

The word *cherish* is equally expressive. It means "to soften or warm with body heat." It is used to describe a mother bird as she sits on her nest. Husbands are to provide a warm, soft place as a provision for their wives. We as husbands are to provide the security, the place of comfort and nourishment. The wife is not the only one who expresses tenderness but the one who also receives that provision. Remember the curse of Genesis 3? The woman was cursed in child-bearing and sub-mission, activities involving the home. The man was cursed in having to work hard to provide for his family. From the very beginning it was assumed the woman would be at home with the children, meeting the needs there, and the man would be giving warmth and security to her. This is God's design—the husband provides security for his wife as Christ provides for His church.

Why all this care and concern? Because "we are members of His body" (v. 30). The grace of God is amazing! He incorporates us into a body, providing all we need. We are one with Christ, and for Him not to provide for us would be not to provide for Himself. And because we are one with Him, He will meet our needs. Husbands, your wives are one with you, and not to meet their needs is to commit spiritual suicide, because you are "one flesh"! Peo-ple who violate this principle in marriage destroy *themselves*.

Paul says, "As Christ cares for His body, the church, and as a man cares for his own physical body, so is a husband to care for his wife." Our Lord's care for His own is the model for husbands. And God has a very high view of women. They are to be exalted, honored, and lifted up. Husbands are to submit to meeting their needs and causing them to be pure and holy. What a calling!

Unbreakable love. Finally, according to verse 31, love is to be unbreakable. "For this cause a man shall leave his father and mother, and shall cleave to his wife; and the two shall become one flesh." That is a direct quote from Genesis 2:24, now in Ephesians 5:31. Time has not changed the divine standard at all. Marriage is an unbreakable, indivisible union.

Why is marriage unbreakable? "For this cause," because we are members of His Body, which cannot be separated. The point is this: Paul is saying that as the Body of Christ is indivisible and cannot be cut apart, so in marriage we are to leave our father and mother and become one inseparable flesh with our wives. The word *leave* is an intensified form, *kataleipō*, which means "to abandon completely." Total and permanent, unbreakable union, which severs former ties and creates one new person, is the design of marriage, as illustrated by the permanent, unbreakable union in the Body of Christ.

The next word is also an intensive form, *proskollaō*, "cleave." It means "to glue something together." The idea is that you are to leave one thing and then glue something new together. It's a new relationship—you become one. And it is absolutely unbreakable. The term expresses the idea of a pursuing love. The hymn says it: "O love that wilt not let me go."

You may say, "But doesn't God provide for divorce?" We know what God thinks about divorce from Malachi 2:16: " 'For I hate divorce,' says the LORD, the God of Israel." God *hates* divorce. God has always hated divorce: and there is no divorce He doesn't hate. He forgives it, but He hates it. This difficult subject we will take up in detail in chapters 9 and 10.

THE MOTIVE FOR LOVE

Verse 32 provides us with the motive for a husband's love: "This mystery is great; but I am speaking with reference to Christ and the church." You say, "Why is it important to love like this? Why is it important that marriage be based on these principles?" Because it is a picture of the church, and this magnificent picture was a mystery, not known in the past but now revealed. The sacredness of the church is wed to the sacredness of marriage: by your marriage you are either an affirmation or a denial of Christ and His church! Because marriage is so sacred Paul repeats the principles in a summary in verse 33: "Nevertheless let each individual among you also love his own wife even as himself; and let the wife see to it that she respect her husband." If we would learn again, in Christ and in the power of the Spirit, to make our marriages what God wants them to be, we could know true blessedness and fulfillment. Approach your marriage from God's perspective. He will pour out so much blessing you won't be able to contain it.

QUESTIONS FOR DISCUSSION

1. What are some of the characteristics of the "last days," according to 2 Timothy 3:1-3? How are some of these things seen in families today?

2. What is the basis of sacrificial love? When was the last time you made a true sacrifice for your spouse?
3. How does Christ purify the church? How can a husband purify his wife?
4. How should husbands "nourish" and "cherish" their wives? What do these words mean?
5. What do the words *leave* and *cleave* signify (Genesis 2:24)?
6. What is the proper motive for a husband's love for his wife?

Part Four

God's Pattern
for Children

Children, obey your parents in the
Lord, for this is right. Honor your father and mother (which is the first
commandment with a promise), that
it may be well with you, and that you
may live long on the earth.

—Ephesians 6:1-3

6

Satan's Assault on the Family

The family is under siege. We have already examined the attack on the husband-wife relationship, and the residual effect of that attack is an onslaught on the family. The effect of this can be realized in the fact that only a small percentage of people in America live in what we know as a normal family, where the father is the breadwinner and the mother is a homemaker. And it is a dramatic development, indicating that we have moved a long way from the plan God established for the family. A closer look at the problem is essential.

GOD'S PLAN

When God originally called out Israel, His plan was that Israel would be a witness for Him. The nation was not to be an end in itself, but a means to an end. God's design in calling Israel was that they become not simply a passive recipient of all His blessings, but rather a channel through which

He could bless the world. Israel was to testify to the truth about God.

The message of God. Deuteronomy 6:4 expresses the heart of this truth about God: "Hear, O Israel! The LORD is our God, the LORD is one!" Here is the great truth that there is only one God. And verse 5 goes along with that. It is the corollary, the human response to the reality of the one true God: "And you shall love the LORD your God with all your heart and with all your soul and with all your might." Here we have Israel's basic theology and the necessary response, which was the message to be passed on to the world.

The means of proclamation. Accomplishing that task required that Israel begin with the commitment of verse 6: "And these words, which I am commanding you today, shall be on your heart." In other words, *they* had to make a personal decision to love the LORD their God with every resource they had. And once they made that commitment there was a second step: "And you shall teach them diligently to your sons" (v. 7). Right there is God's priority plan for passing on the truth about Himself—from parent to child. Then as the child matures he becomes responsible to the next generation, and so on. This was to be communicated verbally. Verse 7 continues: "[You] shall talk of them when you sit in your house and when you walk by the way, and when you lie down and when you rise up." In other words, parents were to be constantly speaking of the truth of God so that it would become a foundational part of life for those in the family.

But the witness doesn't stop with the verbal communication. "And you shall bind them as a sign on your hand and they shall be as frontals on your forehead." Even in periods of silence there was to be a visible communication on the law of God. Here it is symbolized by what they wore. Verse 9 refers to the house where they lived: "And you shall write them on the doorposts of your house and on your gates." So the children were also to see the law of God written on their house. By all of these means the law of God was to be passed on, so that godliness and righteousness would follow from one generation to the next, through a godly seed.

SATAN'S RESISTANCE

From the very beginning Satan's strategy was to defeat this plan of God. Part of his scheme is to destroy the family by disrupting family life. He seeks to take the children out of the family, have parents arguing and fighting so that the family becomes chaotic. He will use divorce, separation, unfaithfulness, and whatever else he can to try to fracture the family, to shred its effectiveness for God.

The initial point of attack is often directed at the father. In many cases fathers have succumbed and abandoned their God-given role. In his provocative book *The Castrated Family* (Kansas City: Sheed Andrews and McMeel, Inc., 1977), Dr. Harold Voth of The Menninger Foundation presents the following thesis (writing as a secular psychiatrist): if the husband and father is not clearly the head of the family, there can be nothing but chaos. He says the father is responsible for the structure and form of the home, for establishing family standards, character, direction, and strength. And if he does not do that, the family is ruined.

Fathers are being tempted to divert themselves from their wives and children by pursuing their own desires, feeding their own egos. When that happens they lose their concentration on loving, providing for, and caring for their family, and fail to bring strength, stability, leadership, and teaching to nurture their family in the things of God. Apart from Christ we know it is impossible anyway, but the tragic reality is that many Christian fathers have become preoccupied with business, making money, or other things that have overthrown their priorities.

And the same is true for wives and mothers. Many are being taken out of the house and into the job market. By 1990, forty-five percent of the work force in this country will be women. Already, six million children under the age of six have mothers who work. Nearly half of all children under the age of eighteen have working mothers. Women are being challenged and intimidated to leave the home. They are often told in college, "Don't settle for being a homemaker. You're too good for that! Push yourself out into the world." There they become exposed to temptations from other men, material things, and worldly philosophies and lifestyles. But much of the failure on the part of mothers can be identified as the failure of fathers to provide spiritual strength and character to their families. The wife is not fulfilling her proper role, because the husband has failed as a leader.

THE PLIGHT OF CHILDREN

In light of all this, what's happening to the children of our generation? According to *Psychology Today* magazine, "One major change is the form of middle class mothering. For a mother to work voluntarily while her children were young was once seen as a sign of bad parenting, a rejection of the maternal role. But, today, going to work and placing a child with a caretaker or in a day care center (or at a preschool) is accepted practice. For many children, that means coming home to empty houses after school and tending to their own hygiene, clothing, and means." (And, we might add, sitting in front of the television.)

Dr. Walter Menninger, a psychiatrist, observed: "We are raising a generation of violently aggressive women who are being formed through children's exposure to television's fantasy female super-heroes." All of these things are geared to change the thinking about the woman, to push them outside of the normal understanding of God's designed purpose.

Our children are being educated by a godless system, and the bitter part is that in too many cases parents don't have time to help their children because they are so busy with other things. Children are under attack by an anti-God philosophy, and parents must not be indifferent to the attack and expect that they will turn out all right in the end. Fighting against an encroaching evil system is a full-time job. Remember, the curse of sin is built into the family. And the curse also breeds rebellion in children.

There is much agreement that many parents, even Christian parents, have failed. We know that God forgives and restores and helps put our families back together again, but we need to seek to live out the reality of what God has willed. There is no place for abusing His grace. We cannot allow the emotional and spiritual needs of our children to go unmet, and we cannot afford to let the world raise them for us. Children are dependent on parents, and no hired person is able to do what parents will not do. As one woman put it, "You will never get your children to respond to what other people do for money that you won't do for love." What began as a great joy often ends up as the biggest heartbreak people ever experience.

EFFECTS OF EMERGING HUMANISM

Today's children have a lot going against them: the curse of sin that affects the whole family and the evil, satanic system that's trying to destroy the family. And there is a third force, the emerging humanistic philosophy, that is helping to undermine the biblical model of the family. Its power was nowhere more evident than in President Carter's executive order proclaiming 1979 as the International Year of the Child in the United States. That year was the twentieth anniversary of the

"Child's Bill of Rights" adopted in 1959 by the United Nations Educational, Scientific, and Cultural Organization (UNESCO).

Many people's initial reaction to that proclamation was, "Great, children need some help." The problem is, however, that the philosophy behind this event was just as satanic as everything else attacking the home. Let me explain why I say that.

The "Child's Bill of Rights" that the United Nations presented in 1959 appears rather innocuous at first. But when it is made clear how it is being interpreted in recent years, that is an entirely different story. These international social planners are trying to "liberate" children from:

Traditional morals and values. Here's a quote from the *White House Conference on Children, Report to the President* (1970): "The real solution requires a fundamental change in the value commitment and the actions of the persons who control the public and private sector of our common life—parents" (pp. 65-66). In other words, we may need a better alternative to parents. The report goes on to say: "A day-care program that ministers to a child from six months to six years has over 8,000 hours to teach him values, fears, beliefs, and behaviors" (p. 278). *Whose* values, fears, beliefs, and behaviors? Not God's!

Parental authority. Again, a quote from the same report: "We recommend that laws dealing with the rights of parents be reexamined and changed when they infringe on the rights of children" (p. 36). One of the things talked about is physical punishment. Under these recommendations a parent would be severely limited in his ability to spank or discipline his child.

"Discrimination." Principle 10 of the United Nations Declaration of the Rights of the Child says: "The child shall be protected from practices which may foster racial, religious, or any other form of discrimination." This "protection" provides that if you are a Buddhist you have no right to teach your child Buddhism, for example, or if you are a Christian you have no right to teach your child Christianity. Children should be removed so that there is no religious influence thrust on them. This is to allow them to be "protected" from their parents' religion.

Nationalism and patriotism. Some of these child liberators contend that as long as a child breathes the "poisoned air" of nationalism, his education in "worldmindedness" can produce only rather shaky results. They note further that it is frequently the family that infects the child with "extreme nationalism." Schools should therefore use the means they prescribe to combat family experiences that favor that attitude. In other words, don't let children love their country too much. Cut them loose from past political traditions, morals, values, and religion.

Families are fighting a very powerful enemy, which has captured the media and is in books, in music, in the schools—everywhere. And unless they commit themselves totally to God for the raising of children, the outlook is bleak. I thank God for His precious Word, because it tells us how to counter this godless threat engulfing our society. The Scriptures are still relevant today because times haven't changed, people haven't changed, and neither has God. What the Lord says today is as current, up-to-date, and essential for us as it ever was for ancient people. We have heard the best man has to offer: it is time to hear God's Word on the family in Ephesians 6:1-4. Only a brief look is necessary in this chapter. We will study it in detail in the next two chapters.

SUBMISSION OF THE CHILD

Ephesians 6:1-3 is the only command in the Bible addressed directly to children: "Children, obey your parents in the Lord, for this is right. Honor your father and mother (which is the first commandment with a promise), that it may be well with you, and that you may live long on the earth." The word used for "children" here is *ta tekna*, which means not "babies" but "any offspring under parental control." Anyone living in the house who identifies himself as a child of that family, at any age, is to obey his parents (the act) and honor them (the attitude).

Unless parents love each other and are really living godly lives, they won't be able to teach their children *how* to obey. Obedience presupposes some loving affection that causes the child's will to respond. It also presupposes a few acts of discipline. I find that my children *want* to obey sometimes, and then in the times when they do *not* want to obey I remind them that they need to obey— with discipline if necessary. Children must be taught to obey and to honor their parents.

The other side is the parents' responsibility.

"And, fathers [*pateres*, which may be best translated "parents"], do not provoke your children to anger; but bring them up in the discipline and instruction of the Lord." Granted, all the opposition makes this a tough job, but there are the resources of God to do it. Don't leave it to the world to raise your children.

Parents need to take a stand with Jesus Christ, make a conscious break with this ungodly world system, and commit themselves to their families. Also, they must realize that no matter what mistakes have been made in the past, God will graciously forgive. Remember the promise of Proverbs 22:6: "Train up a child in the way he should go, even when he is old he will not depart from it." If we fulfill our part God will honor that.

QUESTIONS FOR DISCUSSION

1. Where do children learn their values? Who is influencing the present generation?
2. What is the Child's Bill of Rights? What are some of its statutes?
3. Briefly, what is humanism? How is it changing the thinking of today's children?
4. What is the only command given to children in the Bible? Where is it found?
5. What must parents do to insure that their children will be disciplined?

7

Honoring Parents: The Practice and Promise

I want to borrow an often used story about a frog who was put into a shallow pan of cool water, a pan from which the frog could have easily jumped out. Very slowly the water was heated. Almost imperceptibly the temperature began to rise, gradually reaching the boiling point. The frog continued to sit in the pan, however, seemingly unaware of the rising temperature, until he was boiled to death. At any point he could have jumped out and avoided his fate, but the temperature rise was so gradual he didn't notice!

That has been used as a rather apt illustration of what has happened in many cases to the American family. We have been sitting in what was at first a rather "cool" environment, a "Christian" country that was basically conducive to spiritual things. While we have been content to sit comfortably in the system, however, the water has been gradually heating up. The family is being killed. Sadly, Christian families should have jumped out of the "pan" long ago. When we discover that the divorce rate among Christians is almost as high as it is among everyone else, we know we've been in the pan too long!

The time has come to get out of the evil system that is boiling us, and begin again to establish ourselves on the basis of God's revelation. You see, no longer can we count on the luxury of living in a Christian country where everything is conducive to our spiritual well-being. That is simply not true anymore. We cannot believe the lies of the system. Satan and the drift of accelerating sinfulness have heated the water, and Christians need to awaken themselves to the biblical priorities.

Only when an individual gives his life to God, when the Lord Jesus Christ moves into a family, and when that family is filled with the Holy Spirit, does it then become possible—even reasonable and normal—for that family to function according to divine principles. In a Christ-centered, Spirit-filled family, what is involved? According to Ephesians 6:1-4, the first is the submission of the child (vv. 1-3) and then, if you will, the submission of the parents (v. 4). We discussed these verses briefly in chapter 6. But a closer look is necessary, first in this chapter at Paul's admonition to the child, then at his charge to parents in our next chapter.

THE SUBMISSION OF THE CHILD

Ephesians 6:1 reads, "Children, obey your parents in the Lord, for this is right." You will recall that the word for "children" here is a broad term used to speak of any offspring, anyone born of another person. So we are all children in the broad sense of this word. The idea here is that anyone who is still under the control of or is responsible to his parents is to obey them. I believe that a life of obedience in some sense extends throughout all of life, if deep sensitivity to respond lovingly to parents is learned from the earliest years. But particularly as long as the parents have the responsibility to care for the child, he is considered as one who must obey.

The act of obedience. The word *obey* is a very simple yet graphic Greek term, *hupakouō*, a compound word from *akouō*, "to hear," and the preposition *hupo*, which means "under." So the Holy Spirit is saying, "Children, get under the authority of your parents and listen." In contradiction, the society we live in says we need to liberate children, free them from parental authority. A child must have the right to choose his own destiny, his own religion, his own thoughts, and his own perspective on economics or morality or whatever, they say. But the Bible says quite the contrary. Children are to get under the authority of their parents and listen to them. That is God's pattern and design for the family.

And then in verse 2 Paul says, "Honor your father and mother." This is to be a lifelong commitment. Even when the obedience ends, the honor goes on. We ought to hold our parents in awe and honor, so that there is a right attitude behind the act of obedience.

Here Paul is drawing from the Old Testament. In

Exodus 20 God first gave His law. In examining the Ten Commandments we find they are divided into two parts: the first four commandments deal with our relationship to God, and the last six deal with our relationship to others. Verse 12 is the first of that second group of commands, and it says, "Honor your father and your mother, that your days may be prolonged in the land which the LORD your God gives you." Notice that this is the only statement in the Ten Commandments relative to how the family is to function. Why? Because given the first four, it is sufficient in addition to produce right relationships in the home and in society. This is the key to everything, since a person who grows up with a pattern of obedience and discipline, and a sense of reverence, awe, and respect for his parents will be a person who can make any human relationship work on any other level. And his life will flourish!

God was very serious about a child's honoring his parents. "He who strikes his father or his mother shall surely be put to death" (Exodus 21:15). Verse 17 says, "He who curses his father or his mother shall surely be put to death." All human relationships are based on what is learned in childhood. If reverence, respect, and obedience are learned in childhood, it will provide a foundation that will stand well throughout life. But remember, Proverbs 13:24 indicates that a child is not naturally going to listen and obey. Parents have to use discipline, and if they refuse to do that they are showing that they actually hate the child. That is the message of Proverbs 13:24: "He who spares his rod hates his son, but he who loves him disciplines

him diligently." There must be painful consequences for disobedience, or obedience is never
learned.

So God's basic design is for children to be obedient to their parents. If your children are still living
in your home, whether they are in elementary, ju-
nior high, high school, or college, they are still
under responsibility to obey you. And it is your
responsibility as parents to teach your children to
be obedient. Why? As I indicated above, children
do not normally come into the world ready to
obey. They arrive fully bent toward disobedience!
You don't have to describe disobedience to them.
Children are disobedient because they have inherited a sin nature like yours. The only way they will
learn obedience is to be taught it.

This truth is generously illustrated throughout
the book of Proverbs. In the Proverbs we find basically every necessary element of right relationships being taught. And because that is learned in
childhood, the book was designed to be a series of
lessons that fathers taught their sons. Do your children a favor. Teach them the book of Proverbs.
Notice how the theme of instruction and teaching
runs through the book:

"Hear my son, your father's instruction, and do
not forsake your mother's teaching" (1:8). That
is the keynote verse of the book. Listen to what
your father and mother say. They are not infalli-
ble, but it is necessary that you learn authority
and submission, obedience and discipline.
"My son, if you will receive my sayings and trea-

sure my commandments within you, make your ear attentive to wisdom, and incline your heart to understanding" (2:1-2).

"My son, do not forget my teaching but let your heart keep my commandments" (3:1).

"Hear, O sons, the instruction of a father, and give attention that you may gain understanding, for I give you sound teaching; do not abandon my instruction. When I was a son to my father, tender and the only son in the sight of my mother, then he taught me and said to me, 'Let your heart hold fast my words; keep my commandments and live'" (4:1-4). This is how God wants truth to be passed on—from one generation to the next.

"Hear, my son, and accept my sayings, and the years of your life will be many" (4:10).

"My son, give attention to my wisdom, incline your ear to my understanding; that you may observe discretion, and your lips may reserve knowledge" (5:1-2).

"My son, keep my words, and treasure my commandments within you. Keep my commandments and live, and my teaching as the apple of your eye" (7:1-2).

"Now therefore, my sons, listen to me, for blessed are they who keep my ways. Heed instruction and be wise and do not neglect it" (8:32-33).

"Whoever loves discipline loves knowledge, but he who hates reproof is stupid" (12:1).

"A wise son accepts his father's discipline" (13:1*a*).

"A fool rejects his father's discipline" (15:5*a*). This point is obvious. The Bible says children are to obey!

But children have a basic inadequacy. In fact, because they are children they have deficiencies in four very basic areas. We see them illustrated in Luke 2:52, which describes Jesus Christ, from the perspective of His humanity, as a twelve-year-old child. In tracking very briefly the growth and development of Jesus, Luke touches on the four areas in which children lack maturity and require growth: "And Jesus kept increasing in wisdom and stature, and in favor with God and men." This tells us that children have deep needs in four areas: *wisdom* (mental needs), *stature* (physical needs), *favor with God* (spiritual needs), and *favor with men* (social needs). Consider these more closely.

Children lack wisdom. They lack discretion and knowledge. They are simply void of the truth and its application needed to reach maturity, so they must be taught. Children also don't know how to distinguish right and wrong, true and false, beneficial and destructive things. Such wisdom must be taught.

Children lack stature. They are weak and unable to support or sustain themselves. Parents have to take the responsibility of feeding them and making sure they get the sleep they need. Children cannot survive alone. They cannot make it in the world alone, or defend themselves—so parents must protect them.

Children lack favor with God. They don't naturally grow to love and glorify God. When they are young they may begin to comprehend God, but without proper instruction will drift away. That is why the Bible says parents must train up a child in the way he should go, because then and only then will he not depart from it.

Children lack favor with men. You might say that children are not socially acclimated. The dominant trait of any child who comes into the world is his total selfishness. A child cannot conceive of anything but "I want it now. It's mine." It takes great pains to teach a child to share, because he doesn't understand any of the social graces such as humility or unselfishness. Those must be learned. So children left to themselves are also socially deficient.

When we see the problems our children face we begin to understand why Proverbs says we need to give knowledge and discretion to our children. The apostle Paul also recognized this vital fact. He said, "When I was a child, I used to speak as a child, think as a child, reason as a child; when I became a man I did away with childish things" (1 Corinthians 13:11). Parents, we must provide an environment in which our children can grow in these areas of their need. If we don't provide that spiritual, social, physical, and mental growth we will produce a child who, as Proverbs 30:11-12 describes, "curses his father, and does not bless his mother. . . . Who is pure in his own eyes, yet is not washed from his filthiness." In other words, we will have an evil, unruly generation.

Look around you. You will see just such a generation of young people. They are doing what seems right in their own eyes, but they mock and despise their parents and are in many cases uncontrollable. I say it again, children must be *taught* to obey, and if parents don't discipline their children they don't really love them! The Lord God is our example. Hebrews 12:6 says, "For those whom the Lord loves He disciplines." And let me give you a hint. If you want to teach your children to obey, set an example as parents. If you don't obey each other, they will never pick up the lesson. If you don't know what it is to respond when your marriage partner asks you to do something, why should they bother to obey when *you* ask *them* to do something? Set the pattern in your own life.

Going back to Ephesians 6, we find then that when Paul says children are to obey their parents "in the Lord," he is saying that this obedience is in the sphere of serving, pleasing, honoring, and worshiping the Lord—for His glory. Colossians 3:20 adds a further element: "Children, be obedient to your parents in all things." Now, of course, this stops short of parents ordering their children to do evil. In cases such as this Peter and John set the example when they said, "We must obey God rather than men" (Acts 5:29). When God's commands conflict with men's commands, we must obey God. Daniel was ordered not to pray, but he prayed anyway (Daniel 6:10). Some parents have ordered their children not to worship Christ, read the Bible, pray, fellowship with other believers, or witness. But the Bible says we must do those things. Children are to obey their parents in everything, except in those rare cases when parents violate God's clearly stated will for His children. Then I think they must be willing to accept the consequences of violating their parents' commands (cf. Matthew 10:37-39 and Luke 14:25-27).

What reason does Paul give that children are to obey their parents? Look at his brief but beautiful answer at the end of verse 1: "For this is right." You may say, "But where is the psychological evidence? Who did the case studies? What about the philosopher's opinion here?" We don't need any other evidence or opinion except what is right here: God says this is right! The Greek word is *dikaios*, which means "righteous, just, or right." It's used of God, Christ, the Word, holy living, and obeying one's parents. That term and its corollary are used 183 times in the New Testament alone. God has established the standards for what is right.

The attitude of honor. In verses 2 and 3 the apostle adds a second thought to this matter of parent/child relationships. The text says, "Honor your father and mother (which is the first commandment with a promise), that it may be well with you, and that you may live long on the earth." Honor is to be the attitude behind the act of obedience. An act without the proper attitude behind it is hypocrisy. God is after the right attitude even more than the right act, because if the attitude is right the proper actions will follow.

Two things are embodied in this attitude of honor toward parents. First is the idea of reverence. "Honor" is the Greek word *timaō*, which simply means "to reverence, hold in awe." It is used in

John 5:23 to speak both of Jesus and of God the Father. We are to have this attitude of reverence, honor, and respect toward our parents all our lives, just as we honor the Lord.

But honoring parents also means something more. In Matthew 15:1-6 Jesus interpreted the command "Honor your father and mother" as referring to financial support by their children. He was responding to the Pharisees and scribes who tried to get around the real intent of God's law by inventing their traditions. Jesus clarified the law's meaning and in the process used this same word *honor* the way Paul used it in 1 Timothy 5:17, where it speaks of money or payment.

So the Old Testament law of honoring one's parents meant that as long as a person lived he was to respect and support his parents. Let's face it, during the first half of our lives our parents give everything they have to supply their children's needs. The other side of the coin is that when they are no longer able to meet their own needs, it becomes their children's responsibility to take care of them. Do you see the overlapping of the generations? The cycle never ends. It is God's way of producing families that stick together and pass along the inheritance of an unselfish love.

Notice what else Paul says in verse 2: "[This] is the first commandment with a promise." The first four commandments of Exodus 20 related to God and had no particular promise attached to them. You ask, "Why is this fifth commandment so important that God puts a promise with it?" Because it is the key to all human relationships and the passing on of a righteous seed or heritage.

And what is that promise? Verse 3 spells it out: "That it may be well with you, and that you may live long on the earth." I see two things involved here. One is the *quality* of life we can expect to enjoy. The first half of the verse refers to a rich, full life. The second element is closely tied to the first: the promise speaks of a *quantity* of life, the living out to the full the time God has allotted us. When children are obedient, when they honor their parents, they will have a full and rich life here on earth and live with God for eternity in His Kingdom, in the new heavens and the new earth. In every possible way that promise will be fulfilled!

QUESTIONS FOR DISCUSSION

1. Who is included in the "children" of Ephesians 6:1? What is their responsibility?
2. What is the difference between *obey* and *honor* (Ephesians 6:1-2)?
3. Since children are not naturally inclined to obey, how do they learn obedience?
4. What does the Bible say about children who disobey their parents? Give references.
5. In what four areas do children require growth (Luke 2:52)?
6. Read Ephesians 6:3. Why is this the only commandment with a promise? What kind of life does this promise describe?

Part Five

God's Pattern
for Parents

And, fathers, do not provoke your children to anger; but bring them up in the discipline and instruction of the Lord.

— Ephesians 6:4

8

Exasperation or Instruction?

God is calling us to be different from the world around us. Unique marriages, unique families, and unique life-styles should mark us off from the world. In Ephesians Paul has said that we are not to walk (live) as the heathen walk (4:17). We are to walk in love, not in lust (5:2-3); in light, not in darkness (5:8); in wisdom, not in foolishness (5:15); and in the Spirit, not in the flesh (5:18). We are not to be selfish—each person for himself—but unselfish, each for the other. We are not to be possessed by our own ego, but be under the control of the Spirit of God. In short, we are to be unique!

THE CALL OF GOD

In fact, the Bible has always been very clear about this separation of God's people from the world. From the very beginning, when God called the nation Israel to be His people, He revealed that they were to be separate from the world. In Leviticus 18, when God laid down the law of behavior for Israel, this is what He said regarding the difference between His people and the world: "You shall not do what is done in the land of Egypt where you lived, nor are you to do what is done in the land of Canaan where I am bringing you; you shall not walk in their statutes. You are to perform My judgments and keep My statutes, to live in accord with them; I am the Lord your God. So you shall keep My statutes and My judgments, by which a man may live if he does them; I am the LORD" (vv. 3-5).

Later on in the same chapter God says: "Do not defile yourselves by any of these things; for by all these the nations which I am casting out before you have become defiled. . . . therefore I have visited its punishment upon it, so the land has spewed out its inhabitants" (vv. 24-25). In other words, God is asking Israel, "Why would you do that for which the nations around you were judged?" He continues in verse 26: "You are to keep My statutes and My judgments, and shall not do any of these abominations, neither the native, nor the alien who sojourns among you." And verse 30 repeats: "Thus you are to keep My charge, that you do not practice any of the abominable customs which have been practiced before you, so as not to defile yourselves with them: I am the LORD your God." And God has maintained this desire for separation and distinction for His children through all His subsequent revelation.

Clearly, it has always been God's intention for His people to be distinct, set apart, not yielding to the pressure applied by the world, not conforming to the world. Yet separation is very difficult to achieve, and when we come to the family and to marriage it is patently obvious that we have not remained separate, but have become victimized by the system. Our attempts to be what our society *tells* us to be have contributed to the breakdown of marriage and the family. But God is still giving us the same message today as in Ephesians 6 and in Leviticus 18: "Do it My way. Don't listen to what the world says. You're not of the world anymore, you have overcome it. This is My standard." And unless we meet that standard now in our own homes, we have nothing to pass on to the next generation so they can live to the glory of God.

THE CONSEQUENCES OF COMPROMISE

You may be thinking, *America will never reach that point; we'll never fall that far!* But don't forget history. At one time Russia was a Christian nation. In fact, in many ways Russia was the heart of Eastern Orthodox Christianity, and Eastern Europe was a Christian area, where the Eastern church reigned supreme. There was even a time in China, during the days of the great missionary Hudson Taylor, when the church began to bloom and to burgeon. Now, however, generation after generation in each of these countries have been raised without any clear concept of God or Christianity.

I recently received a letter that helped me to see what may be ahead for us.

Dear Brother MacArthur,

I have to tell you how right you are in Bible teaching. The "liberation" movements in the

United States are reminiscent of the situation behind the iron curtain countries. My wife and I had to flee Czechoslovakia in 1969. In our country, the great majority of women work, and children begin in government schools when they are only a few months old. The impact on the family ties is horrible, as my wife and I know from our experience. The godless doctrine pumped into little children's souls brought up the most cynical generation we can imagine. Most young people do not believe in anything, not even God. My wife recently visited our country and returned with sadness in her heart. The godless system destroyed in great part the will of the people and produced a blindly obedient array of cynical, indifferent, disposable robots.

What scares us most is that the same process we observed twenty-five or thirty years ago in Czechoslovakia is happening right now in this country. The jargon used by "liberation" movements today is exactly what we heard then. We don't want to have to go through it the second time.

We must tell you that this collapsing morality and growing indifference were some of the reasons why we received Jesus Christ as our Savior several months ago.

Dear brother, keep preaching the way you do. We will support you and pray that God will inspire you even more.

Love,
P. and K.

There is an old Chinese proverb that says, "One

generation plants the trees and the next gets the shade." I wonder how much tree-planting this generation is doing for the shade of the next generation. What are we planting to shade our children from the burning "sun" of this evil world? What are we doing to protect them from its disintegrating rays? We are living in the shade of a "tree" planted in the past. Somebody has provided shade for us who are part of the Body of Christ. We cannot just sit by idly and think that our children and future generations will turn out fine on their own—because they won't. Until we come out of the world and begin to be separated and teach a biblical pattern of life to our children, we will have nothing for the next generation.

THE CORRUPTION OF GOD'S DESIGN

Our world does not seem to want to be bothered with children anymore. I must admit I can't understand that kind of thinking, because the Scriptures are abundantly clear that God gives children— they are a *gift* from His hand. A number of passages confirm this truth and reveal important aspects of it: (1) God is the source of our children (Genesis 4:1, 25; 16:10; 17:16, 20; 29:31-35; 30:2, 6, 17-20; 33:5; 48:9; Ruth 4:13; 1 Samuel 1:19-20); (2) Children are a heritage or a reward from the Lord (Psalm 127:3); and (3) Children are to be a source of joy (Psalms 113:9; 127:4-5; Proverbs 23:24). God *gives* children, as a blessing, a benediction, and a grace to life. Children bring great potential for happiness, but only if they are raised in righteousness (cf. Proverbs 23:24). Otherwise, they can become a source of agony, heartbreak, and pain. The Scriptures give us both sides of the picture. Children are a gift from God, and they are meant to be not a heartbreak but a joy. But if they are raised without Christ and according to the world's psychology, the result is what we have today—total chaos.

A 19-year-old sums up the legacy from his parents with his tragic letter to *U.S. News and World Report* (January 11, 1982, p. 51):

I am a 19-year-old who kept a bottle under the front seat of the car the last two years of high school. While reading your special report, "Troubled Teenagers," a single thought came to mind: You can get every psychologist in the book to dig up examples and statistics and all you have are examples and statistics. I appreciate your effort, but just look at it this way:

Post-World War II parents started in the world of liberal giveaways while trying to keep up the harsh discipline that they grew up with—a "free world" and a prison at home. The rebellious teen-agers of the '50s and '60s went to "love-ins" and became the confused parents of the '70s, the decade when everyone went to their shrink.

Vietnam blew away the glory and majesty of the leader of the free world. The economy is shot, the family unit is [in trouble], respect for authority is a joke. For the right price, you can buy yourself a senator or a judge, or he is out buying himself a 16-year-old to use for a couple of hours. The Russians are invading anything and everything at will. Money is worthless, but you're worthless without it.

If the social scientists won't figure us out, maybe they should try to grow up in the world we've been stuck in. . . . Knowing why things happen might satisfy your curiosity, but it doesn't do us any good. Stop worrying about why your son needs a drink before he can face his morning classes, or why your daughter went out and got pregnant. Just help them cope with the reality of it.

Before throwing us into categories, just remember that we have got to run this joint in 30 years when you die off or retire and starve on Social Security. I leave it up to you: Either give us a little help and understanding, or put the world out of its misery and send up the missiles, and hope Mother Nature has better luck with the next thing that crawls up out of the slime.*

THE CAUSES OF CHAOS

What are some of the causes of our present chaos? Here are some possible answers provided by two different sources: a law enforcement agency and a Christian psychiatrist.

Some years ago the Houston, Texas, Police Department published a leaflet called "How to Ruin Your Children," which was guaranteed to be ninety-nine percent effective. In part, this is what the leaflet said:

---

*Used by permission.

1. Begin with infancy to give the child everything he wants.
2. When he picks up bad words, laugh at him.
3. Never give him any spiritual training. Let him wait until he's twenty-one and then let him decide for himself.
4. Avoid using the word *wrong*. It may develop a serious guilt complex.
5. Pick up everything he leaves lying around so he will be experienced in throwing responsibility on everybody else.

Dr. Paul D. Meier, in his book *Christian Child-Rearing and Personality Development* (Baker, 1977), probes the tragedy of children raised without concern for divine standards. He does it in part by showing, in a facetious but effective way, how to raise certain kinds of children. I want to highlight some of the categories he gives and make some observations based on his comments.

For example, Dr. Meier says that to develop a normal, healthy child into a drug addict or alcoholic, parents must do several things. First, spoil him: give him everything he wants if you can afford it. Second, when he does wrong, nag him but never spank him. Third, foster his dependence on you so that drugs or alcohol can replace you when he is older. Also, make all his decisions for him since you are older and wiser than he is: he might make mistakes and learn from them if you don't. Always bail him out of trouble so he will like you. Never let him suffer the consequences of his own behavior.

Further, Dr. Meier says, always step in and solve his problems for him so he can depend on you and run to you when the going gets tough. Then when he is older and still hasn't learned how to solve his own problems, he can continue to run from them through drugs or alcohol. And just to play it safe, be sure that the mother dominates her husband and drives him to drink too, if she can. He also suggests that you take a lot of prescription drugs yourself so that taking illicit drugs won't be a major step for your child. There are more items in this category, but you begin to get the point.

Another category deals with how to develop a normal child into a homosexual. He says to start by following the same steps taken for the alcoholic and add to those the kind of love that guards and overprotects a child, keeping him tied to his mother's apronstrings. Don't let him play football or baseball with the other boys—he might get hurt! In fact, don't let him do anything in which he might hurt himself. Be sure he spends a lot of time with his mother and very little with his father (or any other adult male).

There is another kind of person parents can develop all too easily, Dr. Meier points out: the sociopathic criminal. As usual, he notes, start by repeating the steps necessary to make the child an alcoholic, and add the following: never spank your child—physical punishment is a thing of the past. Let your child express himself any way he chooses. He will learn from your example how to behave: he doesn't need any discipline. Don't enforce the household rules—if there are any. That way he'll be able to choose which laws of society he will break when he's older, and he won't fear the consequences, since he has never suffered any before. Don't run his life, let him run yours. Let him manipulate you and play on your guilt if he doesn't get his own way.

This list is beginning to sound tragically familiar, and there is more. Don't bother him with chores; do everything for him. Then he can be irresponsible when he's older and always blame others when the things he is responsible for don't get done. Be sure to give in when he throws a temper tantrum—he might hit you if you don't. Don't ever cross him when he is angry. Criticize others openly and routinely so he will realize that he's better than everybody else. Be sure to give him a big allowance, and don't make him do anything to earn it. And if he does anything worthwhile around the house, be sure to pay him richly for it: you wouldn't want him to think that a feeling of responsibility is its own reward.

Dr. Meier has a number of other interesting suggestions, which I will just mention briefly. To develop an adult schizophrenic, just show your child no affection, and be a weak father or weak mother. For an obsessive child (one who is so rigid and inhibited that he's afraid of everything), be critical, snobbish, domineering, and legalistic. A good way to develop an accident-prone child, Dr. Meier says, is to fight with each other constantly and blame the child for the fight so he will try to get hurt to punish himself. Or simply ignore the child all the time so he will have to hurt himself to get your attention. It also helps to develop an accident-prone child if you overreact every time he scratches his finger.

Why am I sharing all of this with you? Just to help you see how we have come to have a society that is full of these kinds of people. They're coming from homes where parents are not responding to the divine principles that conform a family to the will and purposes of God. No wonder seventy percent of the parents polled in one survey said that if they had it to do over again they wouldn't have any children. After all, who wants children with problems like these? God intended children to be a joy to their parents, but this will only be realized if they are raised according to His principles. Too often in our society, children become nothing but a heartache.

Unfortunately, that's how human depravity works. Simply do nothing to train your children and this is what results. Let a child have his own way, impose no consequences for his misbehavior, let him rule his own life—in short, "liberate" him—and neither you nor your society will want to live with the product. If parents don't work with their children to help them be obedient they will have a lot of this pain the world has. It's not easy, but we *must* teach them to obey. And the only way we will ever teach our children to obey is to make them pay the consequences of their misbehavior.

If you don't do that, your children will become a grief to you. The book of Proverbs says a disobedient child will be:

a grief to his mother (10:1; 17:25)
a rebel toward his father (15:5)
a sorrow to his father (17:21, 25)
a disaster to his father (19:13)

a disgrace to his parents (19:26)
a user of his parents (28:24)

I think Proverbs 29:15 sums up the whole matter very succinctly: "The rod [what you do] and reproof [what you say] give wisdom, but a child who gets his own way brings shame to his mother." Do you want to have a disaster on your hands? Don't do anything to prevent it, and that is exactly what you will have.

THE RESPONSIBILITY OF THE PARENTS

How grateful we can be that this chaotic world does not have the last word on raising children! *God* does, and He has given us an effective and timeless piece of parental wisdom in Ephesians 6:1-4. We have already considered verses 1-3, directed to children. Paul reserves the final verse of the passage for a word to parents: "And, fathers, do not provoke your children to anger; but bring them up in the discipline and instruction of the Lord" (v. 4). This is the balance of the authority standard that stabilizes the family. Parents are to lead, but in a loving, spiritual way that does not abuse their children.

That was revolutionary teaching in Paul's day. High divorce rates, extramarital affairs, and shattered families seemed to be the norm in the first-century Roman world. Certain attitudes existed that made life perilous for children. For example, Rome had a law called *patria potestas*, which literally means "the father's power." The law allowed the father absolute control over every member of his family. He could sell them all as slaves; he could make them work in his fields in chains; he could even take the law into his own hands and punish any member of his family as severely as he wanted, including the imposition of the death penalty. And he had that power as long as he lived. Newborn children were customarily placed between the feet of the father, for example. If the father reached down and picked up the child, the child stayed in the home. But if the father turned and walked away, the child was literally thrown away.

A letter dated 1 B.C. from a man named Hilarion to his wife, Alis, gives us some insight into how children were viewed. It read, "Hilarion to Alis his wife, heartiest greetings. Know that we are still, even now, in Alexandria. Do not worry if when all others return, I remain in Alexandria. I beg and beseech you to take care of the little child, and as soon as we receive wages, I will send them to you. If—good luck to you—you have another child, if it is a boy, let it live: if it is a girl, throw it out."

Seneca, one of the great leaders of the Roman Empire, said, "We slaughter a fierce ox, we strangle a mad dog, we plunge a knife into a sick cow, and children who are born weakly and deformed, we drown!" When children were thrown out by their parents they often would be taken, if they were still alive, to the forum. People would then come at night to collect the children, raising the boys to be slaves and the girls to be prostitutes. So Paul spoke to a world in which children were se-

verely abused. The parent-child relationship was as
sick as it often is in our own society. In the face of
this perversion of the divine standard the apostle
called for a new approach.

The parents identified. Paul begins Ephesians 6:4
by addressing it to "fathers." The question is, does
he have both parents in mind? The Greek word
used here is *pateres,* normally the word for the
male head of the family. But it is also used to speak
of "parents," meaning both father and mother. We
have an example of this in Hebrews 11:23: "By
faith Moses, when he was born, was hidden for
three months by his parents *(pateres),* because they
saw he was a beautiful child." That is a clear use of
the term to refer to both parents. So, in our text,
we can assume that the masculine term is used
because the man is the head of the marriage partnership, but it includes the mother. So I believe
Paul is saying to parents, "You cannot just leave
the child to develop on his own. *You* are the key to
his life. Family chaos will only continue unless it is
broken by an environment of loving discipline."
Children have to be cared for. As we have seen,
they are mentally, physically, spiritually, and socially inadequate. They need to grow in wisdom, in
stature, and in favor with God and with men.

In a study conducted several years ago, sociologists Sheldon and Eleanor Glueck of Harvard Uni-
versity tried to identify the crucial factors in juvenile deliquency. They developed a test by which
they could predict the future delinquency of young
children. Their follow-up studies proved their test
to be ninety percent accurate. They determined

that the four factors necessary to prevent delinquency are: (1) The father's discipline—it must be
firm, fair and consistent; (2) The mother's supervi-
sion—she must know where her children are and
what they are doing at all times, and she must be
with them as much as possible; (3) Both the father's and the mother's affection—children need
to see love demonstrated between the father and
the mother, and physically demonstrated to them;
(4) The family's cohesiveness—the family must
spend time together.

Dr. Paul Meier, in the book we referred to earlier, says there are at least five keys to the right kind
of parent-child relations. The first is *love*. Parents
must have genuine love for each other and for
their children. The second is *discipline*, a firm,
consistent discipline. Third on his list is *consisten-
cy.* Both parents should use the same rules and
consistently enforce them, so that what a child
gets away with on some occasions he is not being
punished for on others. A fourth key to healthy
relationships is *example*. In healthy families, parents don't expect children to live up to standards
they themselves don't maintain. Finally, it is important that there be *headship*, and Dr. Meier is echo-
ing the biblical standard referring to the father as
the head of the home. A majority of neurotics grew
up in homes where the father was either absent or
weak and the mother was domineering. *Both* parents must be functioning in their proper roles to
ensure success in fulfilling God's pattern for the
raising of children.

The parents instructed. How are parents to

achieve this success with their children? Paul begins with the negative: "Do not provoke your children to anger." The word *provoke* means "to irritate, to make very mad or angry." Sometimes it refers to open rebellion, sometimes to an internal smoldering. Someone may ask, "What do we as parents do to make our children angry, provoke them to open rebellion, or cause them to smolder in anger?" Let me give you some suggestions worth considering:

Over-protection—Smother your children, fence them in, never trust them, and always question whether they are really telling you the truth. Never give them an opportunity to develop independence. In their environment, where everyone else takes certain risks and has certain opportunities, if they are compressed into a very confined area they will begin to resent you. Children are people, and little by little they need to face the world and learn how to deal with it.

Favoritism—Isaac favored Esau over Jacob, and Rebekah favored Jacob over Esau: what terrible agony that caused! Don't ever compare your children with each other. You can discourage a child, make him angry, and break his spirit by doing that. Comments like "Why can't you get good grades like your sister?" or "I never have to tell your *brother* twice to do anything" can destroy a child.

Pushing for achievement—You can push your child so hard to fulfill the dreams you never accomplished that you will devastate him. You can push so hard that the child will have absolutely no sense of fulfillment—nothing he does will ever be enough. Many parents pressure their children to excel in school, sports, or other activities, and it causes them to become bitter.

Discouragement—You can provoke a child to anger by discouraging him, always withholding your approval and only telling him what is wrong with him. I believe that for every time you tell your child he has done something wrong you ought to equalize it by telling him something he has done properly. Sometimes you may have to look hard, and you may have to be creative, but find something for which to praise him. A child responds to approval and encouragement just like you do!

Failure to sacrifice—Make your children feel like they are an intrusion on your life, and that will provoke them to anger. "Well, we'd love to go with you, but we've got these kids, and we can't get anybody to stay with them. It's this way all the time!" Does that sound familiar? Make your children feel unwanted, make them feel like they are always in the way, and deep inside resentment will begin to build.

Failure to allow for childishness—Some parents make sure that if the children do anything that is not mature and intellectual, they are put down for it. Children will say silly things, and suggest silly ideas. But it should be exciting just to let them say what they want, even if it is absurd. If you have to laugh, laugh later, not then. Let them grow. Don't condemn them for being children!

Neglect—David neglected Absalom, and Absalom became the greatest heartbreak of David's life. You cannot neglect your children and win! Be there and be available to share their lives with them. You can't afford the price of being too busy for your children!

Withdrawing love—Never use your love as a punishment, or even as a threat. "Daddy won't like you if you do that!" Is that how God deals with us? Of course not!

Cruel words and punishment—Be careful, those are fragile little lives you're dealing with. Fathers, don't push your weight around or use your superior strength against your children. They can be not only battered physically but also devastated verbally. Parents are more sophisticated, so they can be more sarcastic than children, but you can destroy the heart of a child by your verbal barrage. I'm always amazed that we say things to our children we would never say to any other human being. We would be afraid it would ruin our relationship and reputation!

What about the positive side? Paul says parents must bring up their children "in the discipline and instruction of the Lord." The word translated "discipline" is *paideia*, which means "training, learning, instruction." It is used in Hebrews 12:5, 7, 8, and 11 in the sense of "chastening." That is what you *do* to or for the child. These are the rules and regulations that lead to either reward or punishment. The child is rewarded for keeping the rule and punished for breaking it. To "discipline" then is to train by rules and regulations enforced by rewards and punishments. And of course it's always in a context of love.

My colleague, Dr. Fred Barshaw, sums up the proper goals for parental discipline and instruction. He offers a list of attitudes and actions parents should maintain as they teach their children in such a way so as not to exasperate them, but to maximize their children's potential for being wise.

The wise parent, he says, should: (1) Eliminate all thoughts and behavior that speak of viciousness or vengeance. (2) Reject feelings of anger and bitterness—not only toward wrong done to oneself, but also toward wrong done to one's parents or family. (3) Punish all real, intentional wrongdoing. (4) Never prefer one child over another. (5) Show sin in its essential repulsiveness rather than trying to threaten a child out of it by speaking of its consequences in this world or in the world to come. (6) Never discourage a child. (7) Never promise and not perform, and never let the child's mind become familiar with falsehood and the broken word. (8) Never lose patience, but if the child doesn't understand, patiently explain the matter over and over again, in order to make it plain and understandable. (9) Treat the child as a maturing individual by daily increasing his burden for learning, for wisdom, and responsible behavior. (10) Always try kindness first, and physically punish only when kindness fails. Punishment should not be overly severe, but appropriate to the offense. (11) Never compromise his own or his child's dignity. (12) Treat failure and defeat tenderly and wisely so that they may eventually be turned into success or victory. (13) Teach the child to recognize the true meanings and true values in life. Teach him to pursue that which is eternal, not temporal. If a parent's conscious and ever-present goal is not to produce, through the power of the Spirit and the wisdom of the Word, a more godly person than he is, then his sights for parenting are set too low.

Every parent makes mistakes, and in a family where there is no father and husband it can be especially tough. Mothers often have to be both a mom and a dad. But I believe God will be gracious to give the strength they need if they walk in His Spirit. Spirit-filled parents who instruct their children to be Spirit-filled enable God to make the best out of the worst situation. But Scripture gives the standards, and they must be enforced. And they must have consequences attached to the breaking of them.

The other half of the positive is "instruction." Instruction involves what you *say* to a child, your counsel. *Nouthesia* is the Greek word, and it means "verbal instruction with a view to correction." It is the idea behind the entire book of Proverbs, which says throughout that a wise child hears and obeys the counsel of his father and mother. That is admonition.

So the doing and the saying are both represented. Discipline is correction, instruction is counsel. Together they are a tremendous task, but the end product is righteousness. A righteous child will be the product of "show and tell"!

One father summed it up practically in this way:

"My family is all grown, the kids are all gone, but if I had to do it all over again, this is what I would do:

I would love my wife more in front of my children.

I would laugh with my children more—at our mistakes and our joys.

I would listen more—even to the youngest child.

I would be more honest about my own weaknesses and stop pretending perfection.

I would pray differently for my family: instead of focusing on them I would focus more on me.

I would do more things with my children.

I would do more encouraging and bestow more praise.

I would pay more attention to little things, deeds, and words of love and kindness.

Finally, if I had to do it all over again, I would share God more intimately with my family. I would use every ordinary thing that happened in every ordinary day to point them to God."

God *wants* our families to reach their full potential and not be forced into the mold of the world. God desires that Christian families not fall apart. Wouldn't it be great if we had children who were happy, homes that were Christ-centered, where all these things were working out as God designed them? It is possible because it is promised by God! And when it really begins to happen, the world will take notice of us . . . and of our Christ.

QUESTIONS FOR DISCUSSION

1. Why did God want Israel to be separated from the world? Why does He want us to be (see Ephesians 4:17)?

2. What seeds are you planting now that will benefit the next generation?

3. What is God's attitude toward children? How are they described in Scripture?

4. What are some of the "suggestions" given for ruining your children? Why do parents fall into those patterns? Where can you improve in those areas?

5. What are some of the ways parents provoke their children to anger?

Part Six

God's Pattern Broken— Divorce/ Remarriage

And it was said, "Whoever divorces his wife, let him give her a certificate of dismissal"; but I say to you that every one who divorces his wife, except for the cause of unchastity, makes her commit adultery; and whoever marries a divorced woman commits adultery.

—Matthew 5:31-32

And some Pharisees came to Him, testing Him, and saying, "Is it lawful for a man to divorce his wife for any cause at all?" And He answered and said, "Have you not read, that He who created them from the beginning made them male and female, and said, 'For this cause a man shall leave his father and mother, and shall cleave to his wife; and the two shall become one flesh'? Consequently they are no more two, but one flesh. What therefore God has joined together, let no man separate." They said to Him, "Why then did Moses command to give her a certificate and divorce her?" He said to them, "Because of your hardness of heart, Moses permitted you to divorce your wives; but from the beginning it has not been this way. And I say to you, whoever divorces his wife, except for immorality, and marries another commits adultery."

—Matthew 19:3-9

9

The Reality of Divorce

It would be great if we could end this book with the exposition and application of the marvelously clear and practical biblical standard for Christian marriage and family life. However, we are forced to recognize and deal with the disturbing fact that the sacred bond of marriage is being ruptured at a staggering rate. Divorce and remarriage continue to be unsettling issues, because the wreckage of broken marriages and families is all around us— and the church has certainly not been immune.

The options that confront us as Christians here are the same as those we considered earlier— God's revelation, or the world's confusion. That brings us face to face with the real issue underlying this problem (not forgetting that divorce creates huge psychological and social problems): what the Bible teaches about divorce and remarriage. We have already seen that *obedience* is the only proper response we can give to God's Word. So we must understand the biblical teaching if we are to respond to it and make our marriages and families pleasing to God.

If there is confusion about the subject of divorce and remarriage, it is *not* because God has given us a confused word in Scripture. Rather, it is because rampant sin entering the world has confused the simplicity of what God has said.

The confusion arises when we try to accommodate the divine standard to the *lack* of standards in our contemporary morality, or when we try to compensate for the low standards of society with a higher law than God set in His Word. Both are wrong approaches.

Logically, four basic views of the Bible's teaching on divorce and remarriage are possible. They include:

Divorce and remarriage are not allowed under any circumstances.

Divorce is allowed in some circumstances, but remarriage is never permitted.

Divorce and remarriage are both permitted in all circumstances.

Divorce and remarriage are permitted in very limited circumstances.

We need to determine which of these statements is biblically accurate.

Actually, we find ourselves walking a well-trod path, exactly where Jesus found Himself when He faced the Pharisees in Matthew 5:27-32. They held erroneous views of divorce and remarriage, so the Lord had to reaffirm God's pure standard. That should also be our purpose.

Jesus said to the Pharisees: "And it was said, 'Whoever divorces his wife, let him give her a certificate of [divorce]; but I say to you. . . .' " (Matthew 5:31, 32a). The key to understanding our Lord's words is the phrase, "It was said." That repeated phrase gives the contrast to God's standard and reflects the greatly weakened tradition of the Pharisees (cf. 5:21-22, 27-28, 33-34, 38-39, 43-44). By reaffirming the Old Testament revelation of God's will, Jesus contrasts the divine ideal with its human perversion through years of tradition. They had perverted God's standards regarding hate, murder, lust, adultery, oaths, retaliation, and love. Then, in attempting to live up to their man-made perversion, the Pharisees had convinced themselves they were righteous. In the Sermon on the Mount, Jesus attacks their illusions of self-righteousness and hypocrisy to drive the Pharisees to recognize their sin in light of God's revelation. They had been careful to try to justify their lifestyle. Divorce was part of that life-style. The specific Scripture they had twisted to fit their desire for divorce was Deuteronomy 24:1-4. So Jesus set out to correct their convenient, traditional misinterpretation.

As we try to understand the problem of divorce, then, we must begin with their false teaching. The Pharisees and their followers believed that they were righteous enough to enter the kingdom of God because they kept certain laws. For example, they *said* they did not kill (Matthew 5:21) and did not commit adultery (v. 27). But those were only technicalities. Actually, they were both murderers

(vv. 22-26) and adulterers (vv. 28-32). By affirming that, Jesus was ripping off their cloak of self-righteousness and exposing their system of religion by which they had convinced themselves they were pleasing to God and clothed in the robes of His kingdom.

We have noted briefly the teaching of the scribes and Pharisees on divorce and remarriage in Matthew 5:31: "And it was said, 'Whoever divorces his wife, let him give her a certificate of [divorce].' " In other words, if a man decides he wants to divorce his wife, he should simply be sure to do the necessary paperwork. As with our society today, they said nothing about the morality or legitimacy of divorce itself. They, in fact, legitimized divorce by requiring only that the right form be made out.

They had accepted the tradition of Rabbi Hillel, who taught that a man could divorce his wife for just about any reason (see the discussion in chapter 1). In Jesus' day a man could divorce his wife for burning a meal, putting too much salt on the dinner, disliking her mother-in-law, going out without a veil, or any other reason, as long as he did the proper paperwork!

Before we see how Jesus corrected the Pharisees' errors, we need to examine how far off they really were by reviewing the divine ideal for marriage as found in the opening chapters of Genesis. (We've discussed this ideal already in chapter 4, but a review will help us here.)

THE ORIGINAL BLUEPRINT

The foundation of God's marriage ideal, as yet

unblemished by sin, is found in Genesis 2. God made Adam and Eve and joined them in a wonderful union. When Adam met his wife he said: "This is now bone of my bones, and flesh of my flesh; she shall be called Woman, because she was taken out of Man." God then adds this postscript: "For this cause a man shall leave his father and his mother, and shall cleave to his wife; and they shall become one flesh" (Genesis 2:23-24).

Here is the beginning of God's view of divorce, which is rooted in God's instructions for marriage. No one understands divorce unless he understands marriage: no one will ever understand how God views a separation until he understands how He defines the union itself. The key phrase is, "they shall become one flesh." That means the man and woman are indivisibly joined: one is the indivisible number! They are *one*—spiritually, socially, and sexually.

The verb used in verse 24 affirms that there is no termination point to a marriage. The Hebrew word translated "cleave" is very important because it reveals the nature of the marriage bond. The meaning carries the idea of being glued to something. A man and a woman become stuck together, as it were! When God unites a man and a woman in a unique and profound biological and spiritual bond, it reaches to the very depths of their souls. Marriage is the commitment of two wills, the blending of two minds, the mutual expression of two sets of God-given emotions. Thus, the two become one. Their goal is a perfect unity of personhood.

When husbands and wives realize the truth of

God's definition of marriage, they also realize that seeking a divorce to solve a marital irritation is like a man cutting off his leg because he has a splinter in it. Instead of removing the splinter, he amputates his leg. Such a response would be ludicrous. So is divorce.

So God brings a man and a woman together in a relationship designed to be permanent. The New Testament everywhere confirms this ideal, its most prominent supporter being the Lord Jesus Himself:

> And He answered and said, "Have you not read, that He who created them from the beginning made them male and female, and said, 'For this cause a man shall leave his father and mother, and shall cleave to his wife; and the two shall become one flesh'? Consequently they are no more two, but one flesh. What therefore God has joined together, let no man separate." They said to Him, "Why then did Moses command to give her a certificate and divorce her?" He said to them, "Because of your hardness of heart, Moses permitted you to divorce your wives; but from the beginning it has not been this way" (Matthew 19:4-8).

Notice in particular the last part of verse 6: "What therefore God has joined together, let no man separate." The word *separate* is one of the Greek words meaning "divorce" *(chōrizō)*. The meaning is clearly: "What God has joined together, let no man divorce." To break a marriage is equal to aborting a baby. Both actions destroy the creative work of God. In marriage God makes two one; in childbirth He makes one two.

Jesus says that from the beginning marriage was

permanent (v. 8). In fact, our Lord made that ideal so clear that the disciples responded by suggesting that it would be better not to marry than to get into something from which you could never be free (see v. 10).

If we see marriage the way God sees it we understand that it is a monogamous (one partner), lifelong oneness. So sacred is marriage that any violation of the union called for a death penalty in the Old Testament. The seventh commandment says, "You shall not commit adultery" (Exodus 20:14). Disobedience was punishable by death: "If there is a man who commits adultery with another man's wife, one who commits adultery with his friend's wife, the adulterer and the adulteress shall surely be put to death" (Leviticus 20:10). In those early times God was establishing the highest possible marital law for the instruction of man.

Adultery can be defined as sexual activity involving at least one married person. Other illicit sexual relationships were also evil and defiling, but the Old Testament did not necessarily require the death penalty for such fornication. Leviticus 19:20 is an example: "Now if a man lies carnally with a woman who is a slave . . . there shall be punishment" (KJV: "scourging"). But when a marriage was defiled, the consequence was death.

That gives us some insight into God's law regarding marriage. In fact, God holds such a high view of marriage that the last of the Ten Commandments says, "You shall not covet your neighbor's wife" (Exodus 20:17). For a married person even to desire another partner was so evil that it was prohibited. Jesus also pointed to that evil when He said, "Every one who looks on a woman to lust for her has committed adultery with her already in his heart" (Matthew 5:28). Adultery is forbidden to both the body and the mind. In Leviticus 18:18 God went a step further and forbade polygamy. Therefore, He condemned in a wholesome manner every violation of lifelong, faithful, monogamous marriage.

In view of this clear word from God, how did divorce come to be so prevalent throughout history? Why is it such a problem in our own culture? Genesis 3:16-17 answers those questions.

THE BATTLE OF THE SEXES

We have discussed Genesis 3 (particularly verse 16) at some length in chapter 3, but some review will help us understand this matter of divorce. Genesis 3:1-7 records that Adam and Eve sinned and fell, and marriage felt the sting of the curse along with every other area of human relationships. There were several features to the curse as recorded in verses 16-19 of Genesis 3: separation between man and God, separation between man and nature, and separation between man and his wife. At the end of verse 16 God says to the woman: "Your desire shall be for your husband, and he shall rule over you." That one statement gives the basic problem in marriage (see detailed treatment in chapter 3). God originally designed an indissoluble union, but when sin entered the human race terrible conflict in marriage resulted. The marriage ideal shattered, chaos entered the home, and divorce inevitably resulted.

Prior to the fall, marriage was pure bliss. The man was the head and the woman was the helper. The man's headship was a loving, caring, and understanding provision. The woman suitably helped by her loving, caring submission to the one who was her God-given leader. Her heart was totally devoted to him, and his heart was totally devoted to her. According to Genesis 1:27-28 they ruled *together*.

The Fall, of course, changed all that. The curse left the woman with a desire to usurp the role of her husband and take the authority so that man would have to suppress her. Marriage became a "king of the mountain" contest, with the woman seeking supremacy and the man trying to retain his leadership or using it in an oppressive way. Conflict was inevitable, and divorce became a problem. It became such a great problem among the Jews who returned to Palestine from captivity in Babylon that God finally had to speak directly to the situation.

GOD'S WORD ON DIVORCE

God confirms His original marriage ideal very pointedly in Malachi 2:13-16:

> And this is another thing you do: you cover the altar of the LORD with tears, with weeping and with groaning, because He no longer regards the offering or accepts it with favor from your hand. Yet you say, "For what reason?" Because the LORD has been a witness

between you and the wife of your youth, against whom you have dealt treacherously, though she is your companion and your wife by covenant. But not one has done so who has a remnant of the Spirit. And what did that one do while he was seeking a godly offspring? Take heed then, to your spirit, and let no one deal treacherously against the wife of your youth. "For I hate divorce," says the Lord, the God of Israel, "and him who covers his garment with wrong," says the Lord of hosts. So take heed to your spirit, that you do not deal treacherously.

Verse 13 says in effect: "You come religiously to the altar and weep so much that you put out the fire with your tears: but God still will not receive what you offer. God is not even interested in your worship." Verses 14 and 15 tell why. They had broken their marriage covenants by divorcing their Jewish wives and marrying pagan women.

God responds in verse 16: "For I hate divorce, says the Lord, the God of Israel." God hates divorce. The man who separates from or puts away his wife does what God hates. He also "covers his garment with wrong." A literal rendering would say, "he covers his garment with violence." That is a figurative expression for gross sin. It is like saying you can't ride through a mud puddle without getting mud all over your clothes. It brings to mind the picture of a man who murders someone and is caught because the blood of his victim is splattered all over his clothes.

God is saying that when a man divorces his wife, he has a sin-splattered garment. God's perspective on the subject is inescapable. Divorce is sin, and His holiness responds to it with a righteous hatred.

Even in cases of the most intense conflict and severe sin, God desires a husband and wife to maintain their marriage union. One of the clearest Old Testament illustrations of that is the record of the prophet Hosea. His message is one we need to hear today as our society staggers under the assault on marriage.

A DRAMA OF FORGIVING LOVE

The book of Hosea dramatizes God's forgiving love. Hosea and his wife, Gomer, symbolize the fact that Israel had become like an adulterous woman and was having spiritual intercourse with false gods.

Hosea was to *live* this drama: he was to play the part of the loving, faithful, forgiving God, and his wife would represent Israel, who had committed spiritual adultery. As you read through the story, you can see an ambivalence at work. On the one hand, Hosea seeks to make matters hard and miserable so that Gomer will turn from her sin. On the other hand, he stays alongside making sure her needs are met. So here is a husband who is rightfully judging and chastening while at the same time supporting his wife so that she stays alive and will have opportunity to repent and return to his love. After all Gomer's adulteries, Hosea lovingly bought her back off the harlot's auction block and took her to himself in total restoration.

It is a marvelous commitment. The point to note is God's unchanging love for Israel, based on a *permanent* promise He made and will keep because of His unchangeable character. And even though Israel became a prostitute, God sought to bring her back.

Although Hosea and Gomer's marriage is primarily a symbol of God's relationship to His people Israel, it is also an apt illustration of how to deal with a wayward marriage partner. God's forgiving love seeks to hold the union together. This is certainly Christ's perspective in His relationship to the church, as He repeatedly forgives His bride and never casts her away (Ephesians 5:22-23).

The analogy is based on the fact that there must be forgiving love and restoring grace in a marriage. That alone makes the marriage symbol a proper one to be used to demonstrate God's forgiving love and restoring grace. That is the magnificence of marriage. To consider divorce is to miss the whole point of God's dramatization in Hosea, and the whole point of our Lord's love for His church, and thus the whole point of marriage. God hates divorce. Is it any wonder then that Jesus sternly rebuked the Pharisees in Matthew 5?

JESUS ON DIVORCE

We have already looked in great detail at Paul's marvelous picture of Jesus' headship over the church in Ephesians 5. He is the epitome of the faithful husband. What then did Jesus Himself have to say on divorce? In His day the Jews were shedding their wives rather whimsically. Jesus knew their warped interpretation and thus confronted them in Matthew 5:32. They reasoned,

"After all, Moses said if you find something obnoxious about your wife, get rid of her. Just be sure you do the paperwork."

I believe the error in their concept is indicated in verses 27-28. The context there is clearly adultery. "You pride yourselves," Jesus said, "on the fact that you do not commit adultery. But I am telling you you have committed it in your heart when you look on a woman to lust after her" (5:28). Then in verses 29-30 He shows that no sacrifice is too great to maintain our purity. But with one easy stroke of their pens they were impurely committing adultery (5:31-32).

It was so easy for the Jews of Jesus' day to divorce their wives that they didn't even have to commit open adultery. They could get a divorce for any reason whatever with a little paperwork. (Does *that* sound familiar?) They could quickly shed their wife and marry another woman so that it *appeared* they would not be committing adultery. That helped them maintain their legalistic self-righteousness.

But Jesus confronted them with a proper interpretation of God's law. He said (1) "You are committing adultery in your heart," and (2) "You are multiplying your adulteries by divorcing your wives indiscriminately." Every time a man turned his wife loose to remarry, he forced her into adultery, which made him also guilty of that sin. In addition, the man who married the former wife was guilty of adultery, and the woman who married the former husband was guilty of adultery, too. The result was multiplied adultery! Jesus'

whole point is that *divorce leads to adultery.* It is
sequential, because remarriage is inevitable.

How did the Pharisees defend their perverse
idea of marriage? Their defense was based on an
erroneous interpretation of Deuteronomy 24:1-4.
The *New American Standard Bible* correctly trans-
lates those verses and brings out their proper relationship:

> When a man takes a wife and marries her, and it
> happens that she finds no favor in his eyes because he
> has found some indecency in her, and he writes her a
> certificate of divorce and puts it in her hand and
> sends her out from his house, and she leaves his house
> and goes and becomes another man's wife, and if the
> latter husband turns against her and writes her a cer-
> tificate of divorce and puts it in her hand and sends
> her out of his house, or if the latter husband dies who
> took her to be his wife, then her former husband who
> sent her away is not allowed to take her again to be
> his wife, since she has been defiled; for that is an
> abomination before the LORD, and you shall not bring
> sin on the land which the LORD your God gives you as
> an inheritance.

The Jewish rabbis conveniently interpreted that
passage as a command for divorce! They said that
if a man found in his wife some "indecency" or
"uncleanness," he could divorce her. That is why
the scribes and the Pharisees asked Jesus, "Why
then did Moses command to give her a certificate
and divorce her?" (Matthew 19:7). They misinter-
preted Deuteronomy 24 to say that Moses *commanded* or at least openly approved of divorce.
But such an interpretation is not consistent with
the text.

If Deuteronomy 24 does not teach divorce for any reason, what *does* it teach? To begin with, we need to see that while not condoning divorce, the passage recognizes it as a reality. God also recognized the certificate of divorce (Isaiah 50:1; Jeremiah 3:8). Several Old Testament passages are particularly important in establishing the fact of the reality of divorce. God put specific restrictions on that reality in Deuteronomy 22:

> They shall fine him a hundred shekels of silver and give it to the girl's father, because he publicly defamed a virgin of Israel. And she shall remain his wife; he cannot divorce her all his days [v. 19]. Then the man who lay with her shall give to the girl's father fifty shekels of silver, and she shall become his wife because he has violated her; he cannot divorce her all his days. [v. 29]

Divorce is also acknowledged in Leviticus 21:

> They shall not take a woman who is profaned by harlotry, nor shall they take a woman divorced from her husband; for he is holy to his God [v. 7]. A widow, or a divorced woman, or one who is profaned by harlotry, these he may not take; but rather he is to marry a virgin of his own people. [v. 14]

Divorce is also referred to in Isaiah 50:1: "Thus says the LORD, 'Where is the certificate of divorce, by which I have sent your mother away? Or to whom of My creditors did I sell you? Behold, you were sold for your iniquities, and for your transgressions your mother was sent away.' " It is acknowledged again in Jeremiah 3:1: "God says, 'If a husband divorces his wife, and she goes from him, and belongs to another man, will he still return to her? Will not that land be completely polluted? But you are a harlot with many lovers; yet you turn to Me,' declares the LORD."

In all of those direct or indirect references to divorce God acknowledges its existence, but He never commands it nor does He approve of it— God never places His blessing on it. But He does affirm that it is an evil whose presence must be acknowledged.

In Deuteronomy 24 Moses also acknowledged that divorce existed—on the basis of "indecency." A literal translation of the Hebrew is, "the naked-ness of a thing." Some believe that it refers to ha-bitual indecent exposure, but Alfred Edersheim, in *Sketches of Jewish Social Life* (Grand Rapids, Eerdmans, 1976, pp. 157-58), said the word includ-ed every kind of impropriety, such as going about with loose hair, spinning in the street, familiarly talking with men, ill-treating her husband's parents in his presence, brawling (that is, speaking to her husband so loudly that the neighbors could hear), or having a generally bad reputation.

The only other place in the entire Bible where the same phrase is used is Deuteronomy 23:13-14: "And you shall have a spade among your tools, and it shall be when you sit down outside, you shall dig with it and shall turn to cover up your excrement. Since the LORD your God walks in the midst of your camp to deliver you and to defeat your enemies before you, therefore your camp must be holy; and He must not see anything indecent among you lest He turn away from you." "Anything indecent" is the key concept. The phrase has to do with any improper, shameful, or indecent kind of behavior, which would be unbecoming to a woman and embarrassing to her husband. Indecency here cannot refer to adultery, for that required death (Leviticus 20:10)! According to Deuteronomy 22:22-24, death for adultery was even required during the engagement as well as after the marriage was consummated. So, whatever this indecency was which resulted in divorce, it could not have been adultery.

What specifically was this indecency? It seems that, due to the severity of the death penalty, women were living on the "thin edge" of adultery—shamelessly, indecently, or habitually indulging in sinful acts that stopped just short of actual adultery.

The case in Deuteronomy 24 indicates that if this indecent woman remarried and another divorce occurred or her second husband died, she could not go back to her first husband. He could not take her again to be his wife because she had been "defiled."

How did she become defiled? The Hebrew word signifies "disqualified." She must have become disqualified or defiled by consummating the new union when there were not valid grounds for the divorce that ended the first marriage. What Moses says is that if a man divorces his wife for some indecency or uncleanness as he perceives it, he will create an adulterous situation (why Moses permits it at all we shall see in chapter 10). You can see how similar that is to our situation today—people are still looking for and *finding* excuses for divorce.

Consistent with His claim in Matthew 5:17-18, Jesus affirms in verses 27-32 exactly what Moses was saying in Deuteronomy 24. He says, "I say to you that every one who divorces his wife, except for the cause of unchastity, makes her commit adultery" (v. 32), which in effect, as Deuteronomy 24:4 says, will defile her. In other words, if you get a divorce without proper grounds you will add adultery to the sin of divorce.

Please note verses 17-18 carefully. Jesus came to fulfill the law—not to take it away or add to it. In Matthew 5, Jesus was bringing the Pharisees back from their watered-down version of Deuteronomy 24 to God's standard. In verse 32 He implied that the Jews of Moses' day had strayed also. They too approached divorce with something less than God's ideal in mind.

Let me summarize the things covered in this chapter. God hates divorce, but He recognizes that it will be a part of human society because of sin and thus carefully regulates it. The Jewish religious authorities had perverted the regulation, so Jesus restated it. In so doing He pointed them out as sinners, for they had defiled and lowered God's standard, just as the Jews in Moses' day had defiled and lowered it with their lenient view of the bill of divorce.

This idea of a "bill" or "certificate of divorce" is important to master, and we will discuss that in our final chapter.

QUESTIONS FOR DISCUSSION

1. What must we understand about God's plan for

marriage before we can understand His view of divorce?

2. What was the penalty for adultery in the Old Testament? How does that reflect God's view of marriage?

3. What story does the book of Hosea tell? How does it relate to God's love for Israel? To God's intentions for marriage?

4. What is the purpose of the Old Testament passages that give teachings on divorce?

5. What did Jesus want to reveal to the Pharisees about divorce (Matthew 5:27-28, 31-32)?

10

The Bill of Divorce

We now know that God hates divorce but acknowledges it as a consequence of human sin. But what was the "bill of divorce"? Was it God-ordained, or a mere human convenience? Was it ever legitimate? Those are some of the questions we need to answer. The nature of this essential subject demands careful and detailed thought. Prepare yourself to dive a little deeper!

Although there is no specific Old Testament revelation authorizing divorce, it nonetheless appears on the pages of Scripture, as we have seen (Leviticus 21:7, 14; 22:13; Numbers 30:7; Deuteronomy 22:19, 29). Deuteronomy 24:1-4 first mentions a "bill of divorce." Again, however, this passage does *not* authorize divorce or necessarily even focus primarily on that problem. It is merely the statement of a very narrow, specific case law that was given to deal with the matter of adultery. It shows how improper divorces lead to adultery, which results in defilement.

Unlike Deuteronomy 24, which only regulates the divorce that already existed, Ezra's divorce decree (Ezra 10:3-5) goes one step further and actually commands the nation of Israel to initiate divorce. Ezra faced two evil alternatives: (1) allowing the nation to remain defiled through mixed marriages, or (2) purifying the nation by commanding divorce to dissolve *expressly forbidden* unions (cf. Deuteronomy 7:1-5). He elected to eliminate the greater evil (defilement through mixed marriages, which led to idolatry and its usual companion adultery) by authorizing a lesser evil (divorce). In this unique case, God actually commanded divorce through His priest Ezra, because the existence of the covenant people was threatened.

In Isaiah 50:1, God rhetorically asks adulterous Israel to show Him her bill of divorce. "Prove that you have a right to have forsaken Me." The reply is that in Isaiah's time Israel had not been given one and therefore could not show it to the Lord. Later, Jeremiah 3:8 declares that in the Assyrian captivity God Himself gave Israel a bill of divorce: "And I saw that for all the adulteries of faithless Israel, I had sent her away and given her a writ of divorce, yet her treacherous sister Judah did not fear; but she went and was a harlot also." Jeremiah 31:31-32 further explains why God did such an unexpected thing: " 'Behold, days are coming,' declares the LORD, 'when I will make a new covenant with the house of Israel and with the house of Judah, not like the covenant which I made with their fathers in the day I took them by the hand to bring them out of the land of Egypt, My covenant which they broke, although I was a husband to them,' declares the LORD." They had broken the covenant through unfaithfulness.

Israel had been both immoral and unrepentant. The covenant was broken by her incessant spiritual adultery with other nations and false deities. Finally, after 700 years, God as Israel's "husband" delivered the bill of divorce to her (Jeremiah 3:8).

Now we are ready to ask and answer some important questions that will help us bring all of this material together.

First, in what Old Testament passage was a legitimate bill of divorce authorized? Nowhere in the Old Testament do we find a written authorization, but that does not mean God did not give one. Based on His own recognition and regulation of divorce, and His divorce of Israel and Judah, we can assume that instructions for divorce had been given orally or by written revelation not preserved in Scripture, as God's instructions to Adam's family on proper sacrifices must have been given. God's standard for sacrifices in pre-Flood days is not given in Scripture, but nevertheless it was obviously known by Cain and Abel, because God held them accountable for it.

Second, for what offense (if any) was a bill of divorce legitimate? Based on the illegitimate, non-adulterous divorce of Deuteronomy 24, and on God's own example of divorce with Israel and Judah, adultery was the only legitimate cause, and that *only* when unrepentant immorality had exhausted the patience of the innocent spouse and the guilty would not be restored. No doubt adultery accompanied the defilement dilemma Ezra solved by commanding divorce, but his call for divorce is an extreme historical example applicable only to the covenant nation of Israel and necessary for its preservation. Therefore, Ezra should not be understood as giving reasons for divorce to be used by succeeding generations.

Third, how are we to understand the bill of divorce in Deuteronomy 24? It presents a case of divorce on grounds *other* than the divine provision, thus making adultery the result. As such it was a perversion of God's law. It is important to remember that since we do not know when God's standard was revealed, the bill of divorce in Deuteronomy 24 may have been adapted from pagan practice or as an adulteration of God's revelation. In either case, it was tolerated *only* because of the hardness of the human heart, as we shall see shortly in Matthew 19. And it was far from God's standard.

Fourth, was the bill of divorce ever commanded, even for adultery? Obviously it was not, or God would have given His bill to Israel and Judah long before He did. A legitimate bill of divorce was *allowable* for adultery, but *never* was it commanded or demanded.

Fifth, when did divorce as God's legitimate provision for adultery take the place of the death penalty? We do not know, but the fact that it did is certain because (1) God divorced Israel and Judah rather than put them to death, and (2) Joseph, a *righteous* man (Matthew 1:19), was prepared to divorce Mary for her apparent adultery rather than stone her.

Sixth, why did the bill of divorce replace the death penalty? The answer may be that Israel had so completely immersed herself in immorality that there was not even a sufficient desire for righteousness left in the people to carry out the execution. And ultimately, God was so loving and patient that He chose not to enforce it, as He had done on many other merciful occasions. That is exactly the point Jesus made in John 8:7, when He challenged the Pharisees, "He who is without sin among you, let him be the first to throw a stone at her," and then forgave the woman Himself. There were no righteous executioners, and the Lord was ready to forgive graciously. Divorce, then, became the remaining alternative.

ADULTERY, BETROTHAL, AND DIVORCE

As with Deuteronomy 24, adultery is the matter Jesus raised in Matthew 5:27-32. The Pharisees' liberal view of divorce caused adultery, so Jesus set the record straight by reaffirming the divine standard (v. 32).

A question often raised about this passage is whether Jesus is referring only to divorce during the betrothal period, such as Matthew 1:18-19 illustrates. The word translated "divorce" here is the Greek word *apoluō*, which is used that way throughout the gospels. It is even used that way in other places apart from Scripture. "Divorce" is the most common meaning of *apoluō* when it is used in man-wife contexts (see Matthew 5:32; 19:3, 7-9; Mark 10:2, 4, 11-12; Luke 16:18). Sometimes the Jews said it, sometimes it came out from Jesus' lips, but there was never a discussion about what it meant. They all knew it meant divorce.

The term cannot refer only to a broken betrothal for several reasons. When the Jews used the word they did not have only the betrothal period in mind. Also, the background of this passage is Deuteronomy 24, which is dealing not with broken betrothals but with broken marriages. To take the betrothal period as a limiting factor on a passage dealing strictly with marriage and divorce (based on its Old Testament roots) is an illegitimate and nonhistorical restriction. Finally, if Christ had in mind the betrothal period, He would then be *adding* something to the Old Testament standard rather than commenting on it and reaffirming it as He claimed to do (5:17-18). If that is what He is doing in verse 32, He is out of step with His stated purpose for this section of the Sermon on the Mount.

The indissoluble union *did* begin at betrothal, not consummation, as illustrated by Joseph and Mary. He was her "husband" during the betrothal period. The Old Testament punishment for adultery either during betrothal or after consummation of the marriage was the same for both participants—death—while prior to betrothal the penalty for fornication was marriage (Deuteronomy 22:28-29). So, bethrothal *was* marriage.

The word *chōrizō* (Matthew 19:6; Mark 10:9; 1 Corinthians 7:10, 11, 15) also means "to separate, put asunder." Jesus used it when He warned that what God had joined together should not be "put asunder" by man. That verb, when used in man-woman relationships, means "to divorce."

Three times in 1 Corinthians 7 Paul uses the word *aphiēmi*, which is translated "leave" and is also a technical term for divorce. So we have these three terms *(apoluō, chōrizō, aphiēmi)* which are basic terms for divorce. All of those verbs, as used in the contexts of Matthew 5, Matthew 19, and 1 Corinthians 7, indicate that neither desertion, separation, nor broken engagement is the issue, but the *divorce* of a marriage that began at betrothal.

Now go back to Matthew 5:32: "But I say to you that every one who divorces his wife . . . makes her commit adultery." The Lord's teaching in this passage agrees with what Moses taught in Deuteronomy 24. Wrong divorces lead to adultery. Because remarriage is inevitable, when people who have no grounds for divorce enter into another union, they consummate an adulterous relationship. In a sense Jesus is saying that the sin is not only the divorcee's, but is shared by the one who wrongly initiated the divorce against her. He made her commit adultery. The comparative texts in Luke 16 and Mark 10 argue for the same concept. The Lord is saying divorce leads to adultery because remarriage will usually occur. That is precisely what Moses said in Deuteronomy 24.

Jesus teaches this same lesson again in Matthew 19:8: "Because of your hardness of heart, Moses *permitted* you to divorce your wives; but from the beginning it has not been this way" (italics added). In verse 7 they had said to Jesus, "Why then did Moses *command* to give her a certificate and divorce her?" (italics added). As we have seen, Moses never did command divorce: he simply commanded the adulterous, defiled partner not to return to her first husband. So Jesus says, "Because of your hardness of heart, Moses permitted you." But it was never a divine command.

At this point, we might note that in Mark 10:5 Jesus speaks of Deuteronomy 24:1-3 as a "commandment." That should not confuse us, since there *was* a command not to remarry the defiled person (Deuteronomy 24:4), but no command that made divorce an absolute requirement.

The Pharisees had exhibited their confusion on the issue. Jesus corrected them in Mark 10:5-12.

> But Jesus said to them, "Because of your hardness of heart he wrote you this commandment. But from the beginning of creation, God made them male and female. For this cause a man shall leave his father and mother, and the two shall become one flesh; consequently they are no longer two, but one flesh. What therefore God has joined together, let no man separate."
>
> And in the house the disciples began questioning Him about this again. And He said to them, "Whoever divorces his wife and marries another woman commits adultery against her; and if she herself divorces her husband and marries another man, she is committing adultery."

Thus He emphasized again that God did not establish or sanction the divorce of Deuteronomy 24, nor their further misapplication of it.

We have seen the Old Testament ideal, and it never changes. The permissions for divorce in Deuteronomy 24 and Ezra 10 were designed to meet the unique, practical problems of an imperfect, sinful nation. So when the Pharisees asked Jesus what should be the case regarding a divorce, He simply said that God never intended divorce, for what God has joined together is not to be put asunder or divorced by man. And adultery, which God also never intended, is the only thing that can break that bond. Moses and Ezra were dealing with a hardhearted people when they permitted divorce for less than that. We must recognize, however, that under the Old Testament ideal, adultery would always dissolve the marriage (Leviticus 20:10), since God's ideal law was death for the adulterer. If God permitted divorce as a merciful concession to man's sinfulness, why would He not also permit remarriage, since remarriage would be perfectly allowable under the original ideal law of death for the adulterer? After all, the purpose of divorce was only to show mercy to the guilty, not to sentence the innocent to misery.

There is a tolerance level in the Old Testament that was frequently granted because of the hardness of people's hearts. We see it repeatedly in Israel's history in the lives of men like David and Solomon. Their marriage entanglements, polygamy, and adulteries were certainly not the ideal, but God extended His grace to them. Christ, however, fulfilled the law and thus reaffirmed its original demand.

Does the New Testament also uphold a legitimate exception to the rule of no divorce? Consider again what Jesus said in Matthew: "But I say to you that every one who divorces his wife, except for the cause of unchastity, makes her commit adultery; and whoever marries a divorced woman commits adultery" (5:32). "And I say to you, whoever divorces his wife, except for immorality, and marries another commits adultery" (19:9).

The "unchastity" or "immorality" referred to here means *any* kind of unlawful sexual intercourse. Some say the immorality here refers only to the betrothal period, but if fornication means *any* kind of shameful, sinful sexual intercourse, then it must encompass adultery. Both Matthew 5:32 and 19:9 clearly have adultery in mind, because both passages refer to sin committed by married people.

In fact, the word translated "immorality" or "fornication" is commonly used to encompass adultery. Paul, for example, uses the term with reference to marriage in 1 Corinthians 10:8: "Nor let us act immorally, as some of them [acted immorally], and twenty-three thousand fell in one day." Now is he referring only to unmarried Israelites? Of course not. And when he says, "Nor let us act immorally," is he referring only to unmarried Corinthians? The answer has to be the same.

An increasingly popular interpretation says that this so-called "exception clause" was intended to allow divorce for Jews only, referring it to the very limited sin of consanguinity (marrying a near relative, a practice forbidden in Leviticus 18). This conclusion is arrived at by those who wish to believe that there are no biblical grounds for divorce. They use as evidence the following: (1) The exception clause is only in Matthew; (2) Jesus would not add to God's law something new; and (3) it would contradict the rest of revelation to have here an exception for adultery. That view cannot be consistently held, however, for several reasons: (1) For a thing to be true, God has only to say it in one place, and in the contexts of Mark 10 and Luke 16 the exception clause was inappropriate; (2) in Matthew 5 and 19, it was necessary to include the clause not as an addition to God's law, but to reaffirm the original and correct the Pharisees' misrepresentation of God's law regarding adultery: (3) frequently in the New Testament general statements are made that could in their immediate context be mistaken as absolute, but when seen in the broader context of full revelation they are recognized as an element within a larger sphere of truth. The exception clause providing divorce on the grounds of adultery fits into the body of truth.

This can be illustrated by Jesus' teaching on prayer. Frequently He told His disciples to ask and they would receive what they asked for. This appears without qualification or condition. We know, however, from 1 John 5:14 that the will of God is the qualifier and the condition required for all answered prayer. So, as the will of God completed the truth about Jesus' teaching on prayer, the exception clause in Matthew 5 and 19 amplified His teaching on divorce in Mark 10 and Luke 16.

PAUL ON DIVORCE

We should look finally at 1 Corinthians 7:10: "But to the married I give instructions, not I, but the Lord, that the wife should not leave her husband." The command is no divorce *(chōrizō)*. The absence of an exception clause is understood as it was in Mark 10 and Luke 16. It is not essential to the author's intention here, nor is God anxious to emphasize the exception continuously rather than the rule.

Verse 11 says, "But if she does leave, let her remain unmarried, or else be reconciled to her husband," and Paul adds that the husband should not "send his wife away." If something happens in a marriage and a partner leaves, but there is no adultery/fornication, the remaining partner has the option of staying single the rest of his life or being reunited with his spouse. Here Paul has reaffirmed our Lord's teaching regarding the permanence of marriage apart from adultery.

Now look at verse 12: "But to the rest I say, not the Lord, that if any brother has a wife who is an unbeliever, and she consents to live with him, let him not send her away." As the fullness of God's revelation was progressively revealed throughout the Old Testament, so also it progressed throughout the New Testament to this teaching, which is added to our Lord's. Paul adds in verse 15: "Yet if the unbelieving one leaves, let him leave; the brother or the sister is not under bondage in such cases, but God has called us to peace." Again, the same technical term for divorce *(chōrizō)* is used.

It's very important that we understand this idea of the remaining partner's not being under "bondage" in such cases. The Greek word *douleuō* ("bondage") used here is inseparably related in thought to *deō*, although the latter is not used. The act of binding *(deō)* results in a state of bondage *(douleuō)*.

The same term is used in Romans 7:1-6 to describe the new bondage *(douleuō)* of the believer to Christ, when he has been delivered from the old bondage *(deō)* to sin. Paul reasons that death breaks the bond *(deō)*, which brings release to serve another *(douleuō)* with freedom. If a person is free to serve another he has *necessarily* been released from the bondage of his former relationship.

Following Paul's logic in Romans 7:1-6, the believer's freedom expressed by "not under bondage" in 1 Corinthians 7:15 implicitly demands that the former marriage bond has been broken. The believing partner has been released from the marriage bond and therefore is free to enter a new marriage relationship.

Throughout Scripture, whenever legitimate divorce occurs, remarriage is always assumed. Where divorce is permitted, remarriage is never forbidden. So the Scripture is wonderfully consistent. The believer is not to divorce at all. But if a believer is divorced as a result of adultery when all efforts to restore are rejected, or divorced by someone who does not want anything to do with Christ, then and only then is he or she free to remarry.

Summing It Up

Our only intent has been to discover without deviation what God has said about divorce and remarriage. We have tried to let the Scriptures alone prevail in our investigation. Let's draw everything together with some conclusions:

1. In Matthew 5 Jesus encountered basically the same problem we face today—people who deviated from God's ideal. They even employed Moses to support their deviation.

2. Divorce is not God's ideal. The ideal was to leave the parents, cleave to the marriage partner, and be one flesh (Genesis 2:24).

3. Through the Fall, sin entered every stage of life. Man rebelled against God's ideal for marriage: with the curse came the potential for divorce to occur.

4. God has always righteously hated sin. He expressed His hatred for divorce as sin in Malachi 2:16, but He permitted it for adultery.

5. Hosea wrote of God's forgiving love to Israel. As Hosea restored Gomer, so God will restore Israel. This is the ideal response to a sinning partner in marriage—restoration, pursuing love that seeks to hold the union together.

6. The Pharisees were recognizing and legitimizing divorce for practically any reason at all. Jesus pointed out that they were perverting God's standard just as the Jews did in Moses' day (Deuteronomy 24). So He reaffirmed God's ideal standard.

7. God designed a bill of divorce for one reason

only—adultery. He Himself issued one to Israel (Jeremiah 3:8).

8. Although in a more primitive time Moses allowed divorce and Ezra permitted it to preserve the covenant people, Jesus recognized legitimate divorce for one reason only—adultery. That was God's intention from the beginning. The exception does not apply to betrothal only nor is it limited to the problem of consanguinity.

9. In 1 Corinthians 7 Paul reaffirms Jesus' strong stand for the sanctity of marriage (vv. 10-11). In the progress of revelation, he adds the only other exception—when an unbeliever deserts the home and wants out of the marriage.

10. God *permits* divorce on the grounds of adultery, or desertion by an unbeliever, after all efforts for reconcilation have failed and restoration is impossible. However, He never commands or demands it. In those narrow instances, remarriage is permitted.

Everything we have discussed concerning the biblical standard for our marriages and families presupposes this vital truth of the *permanency* God designed in marriage. A loving, caring, life-long partnership with that person to whom we have committed ourselves and with whom we may build a godly, Christ-honoring home—*that* is to be our consuming goal.

QUESTIONS FOR DISCUSSION

1. What was the bill of divorce in the Old Testa-

ment? How was it used in Deuteronomy 24:1-4?
2. Read Ezra 10. Why was divorce commanded in this instance?
3. How did Israel break her covenant with God (Jeremiah 31:31-32)? Did He actually divorce her?
4. Why did divorce replace the death penalty as the punishment for adultery?
5. Read 1 Corinthians 7:10-15. What command did Paul give? How should it be understood? What options did he give for those separated from their spouses? What did he say to those married to unbelievers?
6. When is remarriage permitted?

Moody Press, a ministry of the Moody Bible Institute, is designed for education, evangelization, and edification. If we may assist you in knowing more about Christ and the Christian life, please write us without obligation:

Moody Press, c/o MLM, Chicago, Illinois 60610.